Endorsements

"This memoir is a monumental act of courage by the author. Victims of sexual exploitation go through an unspeakable emotional journey, which is full of despondency, shame and secrets. Karina has walked through the fire, emerged like a phoenix from the ashes and fearlessly shares her story. This book is a must-read because more than anything, it is a testament to the resilience of the human spirit and its absolute refusal to succumb to darkness." – **Lavina Valiram, Author of *Part Star Part Dust*, Entrepreneur & Blogger.**

"Karina's journey reminds us that we can overcome any past trauma with courage and with the right guidance. It is not a story of victimization, but more accurately one of having lived through it and survived. It is a must-read for those going through trauma and seeking 'light at the end of the tunnel'." – **Michelle Tanmizi, Behavioral Coach and Trainer, Motivational Speaker and Writer.**

"Reading this book makes forgiveness of any kind seem possible. Karina shares her story vulnerably and proactively, channeling the intense emotion of her experiences and turning it into wisdom she has that is relevant and impacting to all. A must read for anyone on a journey of self-love, discovery and recovery." – **Keshia Hannam, Co-Founder, Camel Assembly & Journalist.**

"Brought together with a common cause by the #MeToo movement, Karina is one of the bravest people I have ever met. Her personal story is one of a young girl's abuse and then of a fierce woman's survival. I cried for the little girl and I cheered for the courageous Karina: her passion, her determination and her ability to forgive above all else. This memoir is just the first chapter of a life still to be lived, loved and be told I look forward to the sequel!" – **Karen See, Co-Founder, Embrace Worldwide.**

"The passion Karina brings to her fitness is the same passion you feel when reading A Girl's Faith; a story of empowerment every female possesses but has held back due to society's taboos. Karina openly shares her struggles and breakthroughs to empower us to overcome those fears and barriers as well." – **Stephanie Poelman, Managing Director at Pherform Gym.**

"Karina's story is one that needs to be told, especially in the wake of #MeToo. That an ordinary, middle class girl from an educated family can suffer for years without anyone noticing is a testament to the widespread nature of sexual abuse against women across the world. A Girl's Faith will change you and will make you wonder: who else? A must read." – **Sonalie Figueiras, Co-Founder of Green Queen.**

"I simply love your spirit. Fighting spirit indeed. Truly inspiring. Your strength, your resilience are a testament to us. What you have been through and what you have become defied the odds. It's heartwarming knowing you." – **Alain Ngalani, Founder of Impakt MMA Gym, World Champion Kickboxer.**

"I am writing to you to applaud you for having the courage to write a book on a topic which continues to remain one of the darkest social taboos of our society. We sure hope that your book becomes a medium to sensitize the masses about the harsh realities of incest abuse." – **Supreet Dhiman, End Incest Trust.**

"Karina is one of the bravest women I know. Her indomitable spirit – a mixture of sass, courage and empathy has served her well. She has faced tremendous odds yet continues to slay dragons and defy worlds and, most importantly, speak her truth. Her willingness to open the door and shed light into the most private, painful experiences of her life offers a voice of hope to the millions of women across the globe who can identify with her words." – **Shakti Sutriasa - LCSW, MA - Founder of Decide Differently and Popular Meditation Teacher.**

Published by
Hasmark Publishing
www.hasmarkpublishing.com

Disclaimer
This is a work of creative non-fiction presented in the form of a memoir. The events portrayed are to the best of the author's memory. Each and every story included in this work is true – however, some names and details that could lead to the identification of particular individuals have been changed to protect the privacy of those who wished not to be personally named, or those the author considers would not have wished to be identified. The author has detailed the memories of the dialogues, interactions and facts as exactly as she could although she does recognize that different people in life have diverging recollections of the same events and incidents. However, she acknowledges that the work does not represent word-for-word transcripts of conversations. Rather, the author has relayed these in a way that she believes best evokes the feelings and the meanings intended or conveyed by those words – that is, they capture in full accuracy – the essence of the interaction. In terms of characters described in this work, as well as the incidents they feature in and how they behave, each of these are verifiably true to the best of the author's recollections and are not fictions produced of the author's imagination for at the time of writing, the author could never have any imagination for the sorts of events she shares through this work.

This book is designed to provide information and motivation to its readers and to prompt a reflection of their life's journey. In doing so, the book discusses a wide range of social and cultural phenomena that are everyday experiences for many. It is a work written not only to speak the author's truth in her own voice but also, a work put out into the community, in the public interest. Some of the content may serve as a trigger for particular individuals and this provides due warning to a reader to take necessary steps to mitigate or find support in the event of such occurrence(s). This book is sold with the understanding that the author is not engaged to render any type of psychological, legal, or any other kind of professional advice, direct or indirect, to the reader. The content of each chapter is the expression and opinion of the author and an account of her life's journey thus far. No warranties or guarantees are expressed or implied by the author's presentation of any of the content in this volume. The author shall not be liable for any physical, psychological, emotional, financial, or commercial damages, including, but not limited to, special, incidental, consequential or other damages. Our views and rights are the same: You are responsible for your own choices, actions, and results.

Permission should be addressed in writing to Karina Calver at [karinacalver@gmail.com]

First Line Editor: The Online Author's Office (pashmina.p.writer@gmail.com)
Cover Designer: Rochelle Villaflores Sun
Layout Artist: Rochelle Villaflores Sun / Anne Karklins

ISBN 13: 978-1-989161-24-1
ISBN 10: 1989161243

Hasmark
PUBLISHING

Dedication

Dearest Big Mama,

I wouldn't have had the courage to be the woman I am, had it not been for the faith you had in me.

You will always be my pillar.

Love you always,
Komie (Your granddaughter)

Acknowledgements

This work would not have been possible without the constant love and support from my mentor, Pashmina P. of the Online Author's Office. I am especially indebted to my editors, Max who has taught me more than I ever thought I could learn about writing and letting go of the ego and to Zara for her expertise in editing my very baby that sits in front of you. My deep appreciation goes to Judy O'Beirn of Hasmark Publishing for believing in my story and making this dream a reality. Most importantly, I wish to thank my loving and supportive husband, Eugene, who provides unending inspiration.

Author's Note

The stories shared in this book are based on my best recollections of my experiences. Some names are used with permission, whereas some names have been changed to protect the identity of the people involved.

Table of Contents

PART ONE

Prologue

Who am I and why am I bothering to write this book? These are very valid and reasonable questions. The simple answer is that I am Komal Daswani. That might confuse or surprise some of you because on the cover you can clearly see another name; Karina Calver. So, you may wonder, which is it?

Komal Daswani was the name I was given at birth. But in 2014, I married the man I love and I used that as an excuse to change my name. Excuse? Yes, you read that right. I always yearned for a different name than the one I was given. Let me take you on a short journey of how was given my name and what it meant to me. It might help you to understand why I decided to change it.

I was given the name Komal by my much-loved maternal grandmother. Komal means soft, delicate and pure in Hindi; which sounds like a lotus flower that has just blossomed. Nothing wrong with that; but a lotus flower while beautiful can be plucked and soon dies. I did love that my grandma (Big Mama) picked this beautiful name for me. But unfortunately, it was never a name that resonated.

I love what Komal portrays, but didn't like how it sounded especially when it was said incorrectly. Many people who aren't Indian can't pronounce Komal correctly. They will stress on the 'mal' when the stress is on 'Ko'. When said wrong, it sounds plain awful! No one other than Indians seemed to ever say it correctly, however hard they might try. When it is pronounced like it should be, it is soft, articulate and delicate. And whenever my name was said incorrectly I would inwardly cringe.

Before getting married, I decided it would be a perfect time and reason to change my given name without having to go through many complicated explanations. I found it easier to simply say that it is "common in Indian culture", which is true. For example, you could be Babita Mulchand on one day and then Serina Kapoor on the next; within 24 hours of getting married. Imagine being called one name at your engagement party, only to be addressed as someone else on your wedding day. This, I know, has confused many women in my local community. And it has taken them months if not years to settle into their new role with a whole new namesake and identity.

My mom changed her name after marrying my dad. It has to do with the 'name matching' ceremony – conducted by saints or *pandits* (Hindu scholars or priests). They argue that they know the alignment of your stars according to your husband's name; which is something to do with how happy you'll be in your marriage. I never paid much attention to this aspect of my culture, because I wasn't ever forced to follow it.

Komal sounded a lot more formal or serious to me and maybe to others too, hence it was often shortened to Komie. Most people who knew me before I got married call me Komie and though it wasn't my actual name I was quite comfortable with that. It gave me a feeling or a sense of endearment. It sounded softer, kinder and more playful. The funny thing is my maiden family still calls me Komie, even to this day. Big Mama used to call me Komalie.

I'm called Komie by my maiden family and close friends from childhood. Some of them used to call me *Dilli* or when I had put on a bit of weight (which I did in university), it became *Tulli*, which in Sindhi means fatty (not the nicest name to have). We are definitely fond of the *Li* family. I do blend in with the Chinese, as I am fluent in Cantonese and have grown up amongst Hong Kong Chinese people. Jazzing up the name is simply a form of endearment.

Some Chinese people do it too but it isn't for endearment like us. Chinese people for the most part are more conservative so when they add a prefix to the name it is for practical reasons. So for instance, I'm called *Kay* at work. Why you ask? Because it is easy, since some phonetic rules don't match the ancient tonal language of Cantonese. But saying Kay is odd to them so they add *Ah* to it. It becomes *Ah Kay*. The reason is simple – Chinese names are two syllables and when they speak English, even when a name is one syllable, Ah is added. It makes perfect sense to them, and me.

Komie, however, has a feeling of being teased or stepped all over. Komie is not bold or brave enough to confront others. I have definitely become my new name.

Imagine having a powerful name like Arjuna – you would have no choice but to live up to that name! Arjuna is a warrior from the *Mahabharata*, an epic tale of war, spiritual quests and philosophical journeying. The name I have chosen for myself, after my own quest for growth and victory in the war of my own circumstances, is Karina – a sensual, strong, independent woman who is still beautiful, delicate and pure.

When a bride changes her name, the first letter of the name should be different from that of the original given name. So technically what I've done is very odd, but I liked the letter K and wanted to keep it that way. How did I choose Karina? I literally was Googling lists of names months before getting married. I wanted a name that blended well with my husband's last name Calver, but which also held a similar meaning of my first name.

Boy, did I expect a lot from this new name. I probably expected more from my name than I did from anyone in my life! After what seemed like forever, I found Karina. I tried saying it out loud. I even tried saying it with my husband's last name. I tried signing with it and seeing how it looked. Yes, I took this very seriously. It was the biggest project I have ever invested in, besides writing this book. I wanted my husband to like it so I ran it by him and he thought the name suited me well. That sealed the deal for me. After I got married, I went to the solicitors and got my deed poll done and officially changed all my documentation including my identity card and passport. It was a long process, but one that I was actually very pleased to have undertaken. So here I present to you, today, Mrs. Karina Calver.

Just before Christmas in 2017, Big Mama, who was and still is my rock, became very sick and I was told that it could be her last days I was in Bangkok with my husband during our Christmas break after a very difficult year, so I took the first flight I could get from Bangkok to Barcelona. After a long journey, I made it to her bedside, and saw her gently resting. It was late evening so she was in and out of sleep and probably couldn't see me clearly. I went to the lounge to be with the rest of my family. My uncle whom I call *Bha* (means big brother – he is my granny's younger son), my aunt (his wife) and my cousin and his wife and children were all there and happy to see me.

Through my tiredness from travel and my worry about Big Mama, I vaguely noticed people calling me Komie and *Didi* Komie. Didi means big sister and my nieces call me that as I am the first daughter in the Daswani family. I heard Komie so much that I thought I had travelled back in time. A part of me felt torn between the girl I was and the woman I have become. Eventually, I got comfortable with the discomfort of having my old name back, like an old friend I knew well but had not seen in a long time, and had not really been missing!

So, why am I writing this book? I guess because there is so much about Indian culture that isn't talked about: the norms, the gender stereotypes, the things that happen behind closed doors but also more importantly, the experiences I endured and the way I not only survived *what happened* but have made my life far better than had it not happened. Culturally speaking, this isn't the kind of book that someone ought ordinarily to write. Traditionally these kinds of things are kept hidden, behind closed doors, and swept under carpets.

So what is this thing that happened to me? It happens a great deal in India, to women across the country. You can read about it in the newspaper or see reports about it on the news. It is an everyday occurrence. It actually happens every 30 minutes, according to *The Times of India*. Every 30 minutes, a woman is raped. That means there are 48 rapes per day. So, something like 336 rapes per week. That equates to about 1,500 rapes per month and approximately 17,856 rapes per year in India alone. It is a devastating statistic for Indian society. And, for a long time, I was part of that statistic.

I have lived through years of being raped by my father from as early as five. This went on for over a decade. I have taken a walk through all the secret chambers of hell and come out the other side. I have never allowed that fear to define who I am or what I am going to become.

I have learnt to understand that forgiveness is empowering, and acknowledged that the past doesn't define me as a human being, I can safely say that through my ordeal, which continued until my early 20s, I still have some parts of my childhood that one can call "happy". Even when I was in a dark place, I made sure that I still had good experiences.

I was blessed with being surrounded by so many good, wise and influential people. I've had my dear grandmother, teachers, friends and spiritual guides who have taught me more than I realized. The wisdom and teachings that I have learnt aren't just from wise old men like monks and gurus, but from the mistakes I've seen so many make. These mistakes allowed me to pay attention to my flaws, become more aware and not make the same errors again. I'm far from perfect and still make mistakes, but at least I don't make the same mistakes over and over again!

My wisdom and knowledge comes from the dearest people around me and it has helped me face life's most difficult challenges. It still keeps me moving forward with hope and faith that things are always going to get better. So with that in mind, I present this book to you, with an attempt to share not just my life story, but to go back in time, as I relive those experiences and those emotions. I share with you a snapshot of what life was like for an Indian (Sindhi to be specific) girl living in Hong Kong and how I triumphed while being dealt some of the toughest cards possible. In these pages you will find a series of short stories, which I have dedicated to Big Mama. You will see some of the obstacles I faced because of deep insecurities that grew out of my years of abuse. You will also recognize how I am not defined by my past. I hope these snippets from my childhood will help not only transport you, but give you some wisdom for creating a life you desire. By writing *A Girl's Faith* I realize that the past doesn't need to define me. The experience has given me the pathway to creating the life I choose and desire.

With love and gratitude,

Karina

"No one saves us but ourselves. No one can and no one may. We ourselves must walk the path."

— Buddha

Part 1

My Pillar

"Being deeply loved by someone gives you strength, while loving someone deeply gives you courage"
— **Lao Tzu**

When I was growing up, my maternal grandmother, Big Mama, would visit us in Hong Kong as often as she could. When she was in the house she would change the atmosphere within it, and always for the better. All the grandchildren called her Big Mama because there was always more than one Mama in the house! We'd call our grandpa Papa because we referred to our father as dad or daddy. Papa would refer to the patriarch; the eldest of the household who was more than just a typical grandpa. Papa was active and hands-on with his grandchildren at all times, and was happy to share his time with all of us. He treated us all with kindness and understanding and always tried to help us in any way that he could. Leading evening prayers at home was our daily ritual and it was an unspoken rule that all family members should attend. Papa was a big part in his grandchildren's lives and he was a good role model for us all. Every day, Papa would free up some time and take the short walk to the park. Once there, he would ceremoniously sit in his favorite spot and take out a bag of seed that he used to feed the pigeons. He'd toss the seeds into the air and they would make that sound that only pigeons can make as they rose as a group into the air. Then they would descend down onto the strewn seeds, warbling happily. Occasionally, I was allowed to follow him on this daily ritual, and he would let me join in.

My grandparents lived in Yokohama in Japan for 40 years before they moved to Malaga in Spain after Papa retired. When Papa passed away, Big Mama moved to Barcelona to live with her younger son and his family. Whilst they were still in Yokohama, she would frequently visit Hong Kong. This meant I'd get a fair amount of time with her.

She had her daily and weekly routine regardless of what others were doing. In hindsight it seemed rigid but she had her way of doing things and stuck to that way regardless. She would always get up at five or six in the morning when she visited Hong Kong. I take after her and get up at a quarter to five in the morning.

"Come to the kitchen, you need to learn how to cook *bhindi patata*," Big Mama said one summer when she was visiting us in Hong Kong. Bhindi patata is ladyfingers, or okra, with potatoes in a mélange of spices. Big Mama felt it was her duty to train me to be a lady and one of the many tasks in preparation for womanhood was learning how to cook. The beige-painted kitchen always smelled of turmeric, *garam masala* and coriander powder, especially during times when samosas were being fried. The smell of the pastry stuffed with minced chicken or potatoes and immersed in deep-golden oil would fill the air.

When Big Mama and Mama would roll out the dough into chapattis, I would watch the process in awe, wonder and delight. The smell of the leavened bread would hypnotize me as the fragrance of the wheat percolated into my nostrils. Even to this day, the rich, aromatic smell of chapattis takes me back to memories of my childhood. Chapatti is whole wheat, flat, round bread, and looks similar to a Mexican tortilla. It should be circular, but mine never resembled anything round. Learning how to roll the dough with the rolling pin properly, knowing where to put pressure on the dough, and how much flour to add were part and parcel of my cooking experience. I also needed to learn how to maneuver the dough so it didn't stick on the bottom of the pan so easily. These were all the little things I learnt slowly, over years of learning from my mistakes. Resilience was certainly something I learnt very early in life.

The smells, sounds and flavors of cooking filled the kitchen at all hours of the day, or so it seemed. The kitchen was the heart of the household, where sustenance through food represented everyone's safe haven and place to go in times of need. Mama had tons of pots and pans everywhere to show Big Mama that she was a good cook. The cupboards hid all the magic ingredients, spices and a large variety of teas. One that we drank on numerous occasions was *Pu Erh* – a strong Chinese tea known for its digestive properties. Papa and I loved drinking it, especially when we drank it together. After every meal, I served the family Pu Erh tea in a small, painted Japanese teapot with quaint little teacups. We fused everything together; Chinese tea in Japanese china and, on occasion, Chinese fried rice peppered with Indian *masala*. Our household rituals truly represented my multicultural upbringing.

As a child, I loved making Chinese tea, because I loved drinking it and it was easy to make. But I couldn't stand cooking – even though today, I cook a lot and enjoy it. Big Mama wasn't just big on cooking, but also on the preparation of meals as a whole. She treated it like one would treat studying for an exam. She would ask me questions and test what I retained in my memory. My nerves would kick in and I would often freeze as I went through these tests. She would ask me questions like, "How do you cut a tomato?" Seems a strange question at first, as most people who are able to use a knife can cut a tomato. But when she asked this question she asked it with a different expression of meaning. The 'art of cutting' the tomato was just as important as the cooking itself. She was a perfectionist and over time I followed suit and became one too. Other testing questions would include: "How long do you sauté the onions before you add the tomatoes?" Most people would think, "Does it really matter as long as they are sautéed?" But I was determined to perform these tasks correctly because it would prove to her what a good student I was.

Big Mama also taught me basic etiquette. She had a careful eye for detail and would often scrutinize the small stuff. I vividly remember her instructions around serving drinks. She revealed to me, in her elderly tone, "We all know that when you have guests over for dinner and you're serving them drinks, you use a tray." *No brainer.* Even today, I follow that rule when I am hosting guests.

We had guests over a lot. Many times during the course of the year, we had relatives fly to Hong Kong and stay with us for days or weeks and every meal was prepared exquisitely. Once, we had an uncle and aunty over. They were Papa's nephew and his wife. Before dinner, it was customary to serve pre-dinner drinks and appetizers in the lounge. Everyone sat around the coffee table on the chocolate-brown velvety couch. Appetizers could go on for an hour, which meant dinner would start at around 9pm. Many Sindhis have dinner even later than that, so our dinnertime was actually reasonably early.

I was always in charge of serving the non-alcoholic drinks to the women because most of the men would have whisky and my father and grandfather enjoyed serving that in their fine collection of crystal whisky tumblers. Out came the non-alcoholic drinks on a tray and, as I put them down on the coffee table, Big Mama gave me a stern look and curled her brow. I was puzzled, but I knew an explanation would be coming. Later, when we were alone in the kitchen frying samosas, she said sternly, "You should never fill the glass to the brim because when you are walking, it can spill out! Also when the person lifts the glass up, it can spill too." She then went on to explain the perfect measurement of liquid needed for each glass. She indicated that I should stop pouring when there is an inch of space from the brim. She instructed me with mathematical precision.

When Big Mama set the table, she would treat the task as if she was a chef. She taught me the intricate details of how to fold napkins and the exact proper placement of cutlery on a dining table. She embodied precision especially when presenting food to the family, and details – even with the table – mattered to her. Big Mama was a fancy woman, aristocratic in nature. She would supervise as I set the table with the fine china we used for meals and I found it stressful because it made no sense to me. Why was it important? Nevertheless, my main goal was to please her and seek her approval. I can tell you, she wasn't easy to please. She would constantly remind me that the tasks she was teaching me were a 'woman's job.' In my culture, women were expected to learn how to run a house but even as a young child, I remembered feeling that men should learn, too.

One day when I was about 12, Papa informed Big Mama that his shirt button had come off. He gave it to her to sew it back on and, in that instant, she passed it to me and said, "Let me see how well you sew." *Another test.* These pop quizzes happened frequently and often took me by surprise. I took out the sewing kit and got on with it. I sat quietly on the couch and did as I was told, but I felt stressed. I felt the pressure of Big Mama asking me to perform a sewing feat, but also the fact that Papa needed to wear that shirt! I held the button to the spot where I could see there was once a button and started sewing in and out of the tiny holes with my inexpert fingers. I realized quite quickly that I hadn't mastered how to tie a knot at the head end of the thread. When my mother saw me struggling, she intervened. Big Mama didn't approve. She wanted to highlight that she was the best mentor to raise a good Sindhi woman. Big Mama didn't have a daughter so she felt it was her birthright to teach me, correct me, and make me into the fine Sindhi lady I ought to be.

*   *   *

In my early 20s, my grandparents were worried that I was still single. I was also supposed to be worried because, as an Indian girl, I should have been married by then. In our community, girls were encouraged to wed early and, if they waited too long, we were told guys would wonder what's wrong with them. So the earlier a girl gets married, the better. Moreover, when a girl is younger, she is more malleable. With all this in mind, my grandparents felt it was their duty to ensure I find the 'right one' and get married. Many in the community would sneakily date because elders frowned upon intimacy before marriage. They feared that, if girls dated, then they would also eventually have sex and that was a definite no-no. Girls had to remain virgins until marriage so 'what parents didn't know didn't hurt them'. Those who dated would eventually get married, but I wasn't successful at dating. I suppose I feared intimacy and all that it involved.

Eventually, it became clear that going to India was my only viable option. The search for my Indian Prince was about to begin with the help of my grandparents, even though arranged marriage was the last thing I wanted. I didn't want to go to my motherland to meet some random guy and say yes to marriage, especially to a stranger.

Parents forced a number of girls my age into this scenario. I was on the lookout for evidence that this could make me happy, and it seemed that most of the girls I knew were not, because the spark was gone from their eyes and I would often hear whispered rumors of affairs. On top of all this, I knew that my parents' marriage had been arranged, and I had known of my father's mistress, Sharon, for many years.

I was experiencing an inner conflict. On the one hand, part of me knew that I wasn't ready for marriage, and that this wasn't how I wanted to find love. Many young people that go down the path of arranged marriage understand that they are seeking a person to marry – love is not always in the equation initially. But, as a good wife, you can cultivate the 'love' over time with your husband. For me, marriage has to be about love and mutual respect. Being respected by my husband and his family was vital. Respect from family builds the foundation for a wife to naturally aspire to be more than she envisions and I feared that, in an arranged marriage, I would not have been in a position of respect. But on the other hand, I was afraid of the fate that would befall a woman who had 'waited too long'. I didn't want to miss out on the chance to have any amount of happiness. And so, with a great deal of reluctance, I continued with the plan to go to India.

Before I departed, my dad told me that once I arrived I was going to be married. I was taken aback because I thought I was only going to meet suitors. Amid my confusion, we went trousseau shopping as if I was engaged already and was off to my wedding. I didn't mind the new clothes, shoes and lingerie but I didn't understand what they were thinking or if they were thinking at all. I went along with it because I knew I had very little say in what was happening.

One day in February 1998, I boarded an Air India fight and flew to Mumbai. I was about to be held for three miserable months in 'marriage hostage' at my grandfather's sister's house in Pune. Pune is the second largest city in the state of Maharashtra. There were no young people around so I had no one I could talk to, and my loneliness and isolation were intense. I would sit in my great aunt's house all day, on her off-white sofa, under bright white fluorescent lights, reading and waiting for my grandparents and grandfather's niece to return from their many meetings with matchmakers.

I never had the privilege of meeting these matchmakers. My relatives went as my representatives, with a bio and photographs, to be judged and compared with other worthy young women. I could see that they were deliberately hiding the 'admin' side of this process, the behind-the-scenes work and negotiations, so as to make the girl feel that the guy she'd meet would be her Prince Charming. When they were finally introduced, it would be as if no planning, negotiation or 'offers' had been made: he would sweep her off her feet, and they would live, happily. Despite my misgivings, I'd secretly romanticize about it, hoping that my hesitation was unfounded, that I would be proven wrong and I would be matched with my perfect husband!

I remember on one occasion, my grandparents came back home after their meeting with the matchmakers and I had mixed emotions about it. A part of me wanted desperately to hear that a guy had taken a fancy to me but a part of me felt scared because if one did, then my life would suddenly change forever. I was also afraid that there might be no guys who desired me. My grandparents told me the matchmakers' comment, that my flaw was that I was dark and the men were picky and generally wanted fair girls. That's when any romantic notions I had about the process died. I learnt that matchmaking was centered around matching any single NRI guy (Non-Resident Indian) with any eligible NRI girl that the guy favored. The matchmaking industry, even though primarily run by women, catered to the unreasonable demands of men. Girls like me didn't stand a chance as my darker complexion worked against me. Most Indians who lived overseas preferred staying abroad and found it harder to adjust in the motherland, so finding a guy from another country was a big deal and a girl should consider herself lucky if she did. So when I got proposals from guys who were from countries like Peru, I should have been worshipping the ground they walked on. For many in my community, darker-complexion girls were told they were not good enough. The funny thing is, back then, we made it our problem. I felt that people in my culture considered being dark-skinned like being 'too thin'. The former can't be changed, unlike the latter. It seemed that this 'flaw' meant I would have to settle for any guy who took an interest in me, even if he wasn't the 'right' one. Imagine what this did to my self-esteem.

In India, the definition of pretty equates to being fair-skinned, which puts them on a pedestal. Fair-skinned girls can be picky because they are considered pretty. If you're dark, then what you get is what you get and you ought to be grateful. I didn't realize how deeply it affected me subconsciously until I started dating – I wouldn't put myself first because I didn't see myself as an equal. I was made to feel that my complexion had put me in a lower category. How we, as Indians, discuss complexion can irreversibly damage how girls view themselves.

As well as waiting around for my envoys to return from their matchmaking duties, my days also consisted of shopping for fabrics with Big Mama. She was very image-conscious, so getting her Indian outfits custom-made was important, and indeed portrayed her desire to always be unique. She would include me in her fashion decisions, much to my discomfort, as I truly didn't see what there was to get excited about in fashion and tailoring. She would allow me to choose fabric for my outfits, and part of the decision-making process was to choose the neck design for a salwar kameez. One day, she asked me which one I wanted, and I pointed to the same style I always chose. She didn't say anything, just made a face and shook her head. I could tell she thought I was far less stylish than I should have been!

During the three months in Pune, I had to practice cooking. By now, it had been drilled into me that the main job of a wife is to feed their husband, so the way to a man's heart is (obviously) through food. I hadn't been good at a number of recipes, ever since my childhood chapatti fiascos. Another basic dish I was scared of making was an omelet because I didn't know how to flip an egg, and an omelet just looked so much harder. Whenever I did try flipping an egg, it would end up on the floor in an unholy state.

After what felt like forever in India, an aunt I call Didi (which means big sister) visited with her son, who was probably two or three years old. I met this didi previously when she came to Hong Kong for a holiday before she got married. I remember loving her on this visit, and I was so excited to see her again.

Even today, Didi Mana is the sweetest and most gorgeous woman I have ever encountered. So, I felt very relieved when she visited Pune because I had felt quite trapped and hadn't spoken to someone 'cool' for the longest time. Having someone to talk to would be a massive relief. And of course, in the late 90s the Internet wasn't a big phenomenon and I didn't even own a mobile phone, so my social life for three months had been at a complete standstill.

One day, Didi Mana was busy feeding her little boy and wanted to have something easy to eat. That's when Big Mama turned and told me to make Didi Mana an omelet. I froze. I wanted to dig a hole and bury myself. "She didn't say omelet, did she?" I was thinking out loud, under my breath so Big Mama couldn't hear. I panicked. Why did she think I could make an omelet? In my grandmother's eyes, I was at a marriageable age, so clearly my cooking skills would or should have been at a decent standard.

She might have been able to see the fear written plainly on my face, or she might have heard me with her precise hearing, so because Big Mama didn't want me to be embarrassed, she took me to the kitchen and asked me to cut the vegetables – onion, tomatoes and coriander. I obeyed without uttering a word. I knew that making an omelet was very basic and was ashamed I hadn't managed to learn how. Taking pity on me, it seemed, she then showed me how it was done. She broke two eggs in a bowl, whisked them with a bit of milk and added the vegetables, salt and pepper. She added oil to the frying pan. She waited patiently until the pan was hot. She poured the mixture into the pan. She let it sit for a few minutes, then flipped it over like a chef. I watched in amazement at her culinary skills. Once it was done, she placed it on a plate and told me to toast two slices of bread and serve it to Didi Mana. I felt so grateful for her kind instruction, and I never forgot how to make an omelet after that.

Big Mama was consistently good at observing how things were done. She kept a careful eye on how tasks were being performed. She once told me to clean the dining table after lunch. It had a tablecloth with a plastic cover, so I used a wet cloth to clean it. She would be nowhere in sight, or so I would think, but actually she was watching every little chore I was doing. She was on duty even when she was not. After cleaning the table, she summoned me and told me that I had to clean the table again because I had missed bits of crumbs. I sheepishly went back to the kitchen, got the wet cloth, and picked up the remaining crumbs. Then I retrieved the dry cloth from the kitchen, and dried off the table. After many attempts, I learnt Big Mama's trick: I had to bend down and look at the table from another angle so I could see the crumbs that weren't visible to the naked eye when standing over the table. To this day, I check for crumbs on tables or counters this way. Another part of her is in me.

Other than cooking and domestic chores, she was also committed to prayers and rituals. She would meditate, have her tea, and then come into my bedroom where the prayer room was set up. On some weekends, she'd wake me up and tell me to join her in the rituals.

Big Mama had figurines and framed pictures of the Hindu Gods on her altar, and her routine involved cleaning the small statues first. We would start with placing the silver figurines' clothes in a row and then she would give them a bath. The bath consisted of using a stainless steel bowl and a stainless steel glass, which was filled with water. Each figurine would be bathed individually, and then she would give them to me to dry off with a cloth. After the bath, she asked me to arrange the clothes separately for each one. These little figurines had plenty of pretty outfits that Big Mama had made by hand. I would get to pick the outfit and all of them wore the same set. The clothes were always colorful and sparkly, just like her personality. She would usually take one of the figurines and show me how to dress it up because some of them were a lot more complicated than the others. I found this part the most enjoyable because I was playing dress-up with someone I admired, plus with the Gods. It couldn't get any better!

After they got new clothes to wear, the figurines were placed back where they belonged on the altar. Next, she marked each statue with sandalwood *tilak*, which is made from sandalwood paste and placed on the center of the forehead. She would do this for all the framed Gods and Goddesses as well. We had a lot of pictures in the prayer room. I watched her and I'd help by putting the tilak on the Gods and Goddesses' foreheads – it had to be done perfectly. We used our wedding finger and the tilak had to be a circle so getting it right was tricky. Hers were always flawless. Mine would be either three-fourths right or the paste would start running down the pictures or figurines, and I'd have to wipe it down and do it again.

Big Mama would chant when she did her rituals as an offering to the Lord. I didn't think much about it then, but, today, I love chants and I now understand that it came from her teachings. I chant now as a form of purification and connecting to Source. We ended by singing some prayers. After that she would make her way to the lounge and have breakfast.

On days when I was still in bed snoring away, she would ring the bell that she used during the *aarti* (religious ritual worship, a part of *puja* (prayer), in which light from wicks soaked in *ghee* (purified butter) or camphor is offered to one or more deities) or, at times, she'd wake me up because clearly it was late and a girl should be up by a certain time.

My family had a lot of rules for how a girl should or should not behave. It was something Big Mama lived by and believed it made me a better woman. I think she did what she could to give me a leg up in life – because no Indian man would want a woman who didn't know how to perform rituals. But more than giving me a leg up, she gave me faith and taught me how to connect with God, which, again, became evident as I transformed into an adult and went through my own trials and tribulations.

Big Mama felt that the way I behaved in society reflected upon her so she would constantly critique my behavior to guide me to be the best version of myself. This is something I live by; though different from the rules I thought I should live by back then. Nevertheless, being the best version of myself allows me to push myself, to be open to criticism and to commit to what I am focusing on.

In my opinion, Sindhis are a lot more closed-minded about breaking away from our tight-knit society. It might sound a little judgmental, but what I am trying to say is we prefer marrying our own kind. When I say 'our own kind', I don't mean just Indians but our own ethnicity. It seems to be for a few reasons: Firstly, marrying our own is easier because we have had a similar upbringing, language, diet, religious rituals and therefore it's meant to be easier for us to get along. The idea is that, if the basic commonality is the same, then there will be less conflict in the marriage. And while the intention is pure, it doesn't always work for Sindhis who are integrated into another culture and lifestyle. Take me as an example: being Sindhi, my natural first language should be Sindhi but English became my first language. My religious background was Hindu but I didn't feel very connected to Hinduism, and much later converted to Buddhism as it better fits who I am. While I love Indian food, I couldn't eat it every day and would choose Chinese cuisine over Indian in a heartbeat. Even though I am Indian, I don't see myself as a typical Indian. If I married an Indian, the basic foundation of commonality that works for many wouldn't work for me.

The month of my 23rd birthday, and after three months spent waiting in Pune, I had to go home. My visa had expired, and I carried with me a string of rejections from potential 'good' suitors, but to my credit, I had also done my share of saying "no, thanks". The final round of matchmakers had spoken to my father on the phone, and told him that I was a lost cause – they couldn't find a match for me. My father and his parents were devastated, and I had some very mixed feelings. While I felt the effects of months of being judged, measured and compared, I was also relieved to be going home. I worried that this would be a recurring element for me, and that perhaps I was just not good enough. Was I ever going to find love?

I can't help wondering what might have happened if that trip had proven fruitful, and Big Mama's orders to find me a husband had led to a marriage. I also suspect that there was an element of bluffing on the part of my father: Indian weddings are expensive, and I don't know that he would have been able to afford a lavish five-day affair. Later that same year, my father announced that he was leaving our family. He now lives with his mistress of many years, Sharon, together with their daughter who was born when I was a young teen.

*   *   *

Fifteen years later, when I called Big Mama to tell her I was engaged, I was terrified. Terrified because, in my mind, she was still a traditional Indian woman who believed in customs that I still didn't understand and I was about to tell her about my engagement – to a foreigner (gasp!). Behind closed doors – away from her watchful eyes – my cousins and I would jokingly call her 'headquarters'. That meant we would need to get approval from her for big things in our life like travelling, whom we married and how we conducted ourselves inside and outside the family home. To be honest, I felt that she was 'headquarters' to me for almost everything, from my high-school grades, to which guy I married, or how I dressed. Imagine my anxiety when I told her this huge news – that I would be marrying out of my culture, nationality and caste!

One weekend, I made the big phone call. My Bha (my father's brother) answered. I just blurted it out at him, and he was immediately thrilled. I'm glad he got to hear it first, because it gave me a chance to steady my nerves. I asked him to pass the phone to Big Mama. I remember saying, "Big Mama, I'm engaged."

She was over the moon! But before she could get too excited, I stopped her and said, "He is British."

She said, "I know."

I was puzzled. "Did she hear me?" I wondered.

"Big Mama, he is white." I emphasized. I wanted to make absolutely sure she understood me.

To ensure I knew exactly what she meant, she replied, "I saw his picture. He is very handsome and has a kind face."

That comment melted my heart. She approved! I was beaming. The irony was that my immediate family didn't seem as excited as she was initially, even though I considered her the most traditional person in the whole family. I couldn't help but wonder what brought about this change in Big Mama. Much later, I realized that my Papa's passing contributed to her becoming more flexible about how we did things or what we did as long as we were happy.

Whenever she asked about my husband she would inquire, "Are you happy? How is your Prince?" It was so comforting to hear this from her because it meant that to her, all that mattered was that I was happy. My joy was all she cared about and I always felt so warm feeling that from her.

After we got married in the summer of 2014, my husband and I traveled to Barcelona and that was the first time Big Mama met the man I had chosen to marry. I was excited, but also a bit nervous. I knew she was overjoyed that we had got married, but she hadn't met him yet so I was still slightly apprehensive. We didn't have the typical five-day

Indian wedding because that wasn't something we wanted. We exchanged our vows at the Marriage Registry in Hong Kong and, after the signing, we had a simple family meal. We wanted to keep our wedding celebrations small and have an adventurous honeymoon rather than spending a lot on a lavish wedding. Due to the nature of our small wedding, Big Mama didn't come and we thought there was no need for her to fly all the way to Hong Kong. So, instead, we went to Barcelona two months afterwards.

The moment she saw us, she smiled from cheek to cheek. It melted my heart to see my husband and Big Mama get on so well, especially when my husband doesn't speak Sindhi or Hindi and her English was limited. It showed me that the language of love is far greater than any words can say. She would sit with him on the couch and they would watch *Two and a Half Men*. My husband didn't really watch TV at home and I had no idea that Big Mama liked this sitcom! Growing up, she barely watched TV during the day, so the changes in her were all very new to me. I was wrapped up playing and spending time with my nieces that I didn't notice what Big Mama and my husband were up to. They'd laugh and talk about *Two and a Half Men*. How cute was that?!

*   *   *

On the morning of May 10th, 2018, at 4.30am when I was checking my phone, I saw a message from my Bha, he wrote "our beloved Mummy left for heavenly abode at 8.30pm. May God rest her soul in Eternal Peace."

Immediately, I started sobbing. I was distraught and couldn't catch my breath. I had known she was going to go soon, but it didn't make it any easier to receive the news. When I saw her over Christmas, she was bedridden and I was told she was going to go soon. I flew to Barcelona from Bangkok, and cut my holiday short to be with my sweet Big Mama. Knowing that she was going to pass on soon, and having her actually gone, were two very different realities. I felt like my whole world stopped because she was the one person from whom I learnt the most of what I now know. I was not her daughter, but Big Mama took an interest in me, teaching me, sometimes forcefully, things she thought would help me in some way, shape or form. Losing her felt like losing the one person who stood by me no matter what.

I truly believe she is in the Pure Land. I do pray she is. The Pure Land is similar to heaven, and is, according to Buddhists, the realm of Gods and Angels. She's happy there and I am happy for her. I've lost her physically and that was heartbreaking. Accepting that I won't get a phone call on my birthday or that, when I go to Barcelona, she will no longer be there or that, when I video chat with my family in Barcelona, I will not see her, felt like a void had been seared into my heart. It was a sudden realization that I was going to lose all of that. While I no longer will have any more physical moments with her, I have lots of memories of her that I hold dearly in my heart. After all, she was and will constantly remain the strongest pillar in my life.

In Search Of My Yin

"Never ever accept 'Because You Are a Woman' as a reason for doing or not doing anything."
— **Chimamanda Adichie**

As an infant, tears would cascade down my dark face when my mom would rub *besan paste* on my tiny fragile body. The paste was made from chickpeas, flour, yogurt, lemon juice and a pinch of turmeric then rubbed vigorously onto my skin until it hurt. The scrubbing seemed symbolic of trying to remove my 'darkness' from the outside because being dark was considered a sin, and there was no pride attached to the way I was born with dusky skin and thick black hair all over my body. "Oh Bhagwan (Oh Lord), we can't have a girl who's hairy and dark. Who will marry her?" I could hear my mom saying to my grandma every time the besan paste would be lathered harshly onto my skin. Vigorous rubbing and sighs from my mother left me feeling helpless.

I looked the complete opposite of how beauty was perceived. Barbie is the perfect image of how a girl *should* look. Playing dress up with my Barbie dolls was my escapism into a world where I was like an Indian version of a Barbie. I admired her beauty and it made me feel feminine when I was a child. Her perfect body, lipstick and clothes surrounded me with comforting images of womanhood. Rejecting my looks and body to shun my feminine side became a big part of my life at a very young age. In my teenage years, the shackles of these stereotypes deeply affected me when I slowly began to truly unravel the concept of femininity.

Vulnerability, elegance, 'getting dolled up' and nurturing offspring became my idea of femininity. It is really the Yin to the Yang; an ancient Chinese philosophy describes the practice of polar opposites of masculine and feminine energies connecting to make a whole. In my younger days, the concept of the law of polarity and magnetic forces creating fusion were as foreign to me as the Chinese language is to a Greek person. Searching for my Yin became much harder for me to find completely as a child, because in a way my femininity had been robbed. The sad truth is that through the years of the abuse, my desire to be feminine was clouded, because being womanly reminded me of my father's mistress, Sharon, and the abuse I endured at his hands.

Primary school was a terrible time for my body and keeping up my outside appearance. The local government primary school I attended in Hong Kong already branded me a minority because I was different. My dark complexion and thick black hair braided into a ponytail every day did not mirror the local Chinese children who had porcelain white skin and straight rigid bob haircuts. My difference stood out like a sore thumb, which made me an automatic outsider, drawing unwanted and unwarranted attention – especially my hairy legs and arms. The boys used to tease me because body hair made me look masculine. When I was harassed, thoughts of being feminine and craving to look like the other Chinese girls created inadequacy and insecurities in how I perceived myself.

Waxing didn't come into my life until much later. During lessons at school, students were required to raise their hand to garner attention from the teacher. I tried not to raise my arms too high, for fear of the jungle under my arm being revealed to the whole class. With 44 students in the class, it was almost impossible to avoid bullying if anyone noticed the forest of thick, jet-black hair growing under my arm.

And then it happened in one particular lesson, when I raised my hand a bit higher than I meant to, and the hair poked out of my sleeveless uniform. The sneers and laughter from the classroom sent me into a fury wondering why the stupid uniform was designed with cropped sleeves. I heard a few of the girls also comment on my skin tone and embarrassment crept up from my toes all the way to my head, as the hot tears started to form on the sides of my eyes. On that day at school I felt so ashamed and unfeminine. I went through primary school trying to ignore the shame of my heritage. I pushed away my feelings of vulnerability and soldiered on, fiercely pretending to be unaffected.

Positive role models never surrounded me. Sharon, the woman I came to know initially as my father's friend or his client, but later found out was his mistress, presented a skewed image of femininity. She made me feel that her looks and demeanor were solely used to attract the opposite gender. Sharon wore short skirts, heavy makeup and her dress sense mirrored my image of a prostitute. Watching her behave in an overly feminine and sensual way in front of my father made me want to do the opposite in regards to my posture, demeanor, clothes and the way I walked. Instead of walking with grace and pride, adopting a sluggish stagger suited me more, as a means of protection from being exceedingly womanly in front of my father. This was a protective mechanism to arm me with strength that grossly over-inflated the Yang side of me. My purposeful disconnection from Sharon and her feminine side pushed me further towards becoming a 'boyish' rendition of myself. Although I knew I was a girl, the disconnection from my Yin created an immense gap between the way I looked and felt.

In my teenage years, waxing was meant to save my life. Everyone started waxing in their teens – even though it was as painful as giving birth, apparently. All the girls I knew did it. Going to the parlor, or when the beautician came to my house, made me feel nauseous and at each waxing session I would stand still as each hair follicle was pulled violently from my skin, with a thick sticky honey-like mixture. Every time, I was subjected to the longest two hours of my life. Sweat would begin trickling down my neck, until I was lying in a puddle of my own bodily fluids. Even with the air conditioner on full blast, I hated the cold anxiety of the wax touching my skin. My cortisol levels would skyrocket, and I would have to think of methods to keep calm without getting dizzy and nauseous.

I vividly recall one time, the beautician who I saw as a monstrous, agony-inducing person walked into the room and I knew I was about to experience a world of pain. She had everything set out; the wax concoction, the butter knife she used to apply the wax, cloth to pull the wax, baby powder and a wet towel. She was ready and I was hesitant. I laid on my bed shaking with my bare legs covered with a duvet. She gently applied a layer of sticky looking mixture on my leg and then placed a long thin white cloth over it, so she could yank it out with all her might. I wondered if she relished the pain we girls go through. As she massaged the white cloth, I was hoping that magically by rubbing the cloth, the hair from its follicles would come off without her vigorous pull. But to my disappointment, I wasn't off the hook; the yank was about to happen. I laid on my bed, holding the ends of the bed, as she went for the cloth. "Oooooooouch!" I yelled so loudly, it seemed to have burst her eardrums. I screamed for Mama and demanded that the waxer leave. I proclaimed that I would rather have patches of hair on my leg than this level of torture for another two hours. My mom had no choice but to give up on me.

I finally won the battle and out came the razor and blades. The sharp blade would cut my skin as if to indicate that I didn't deserve to look beautiful. I resorted to blades as if to remind myself that I wasn't worthy of smooth silky skin. I didn't need to look attractive because my complexion subjected me to feeling inferior. Yes, I know it's awful to shave and it ruins your skin but you can't be in high school and have hairy legs. Shaving became my ally and I religiously used it when the roots started to prick me. I never completely understood why women made body hair our enemy and why we went to such lengths to be free from it. I understand to some extent that being free feels good but what does that say about the disparity between men and women? Some ethnicities in India are hairier than the others and that is regardless of gender. My community constantly enforced that women should feel and look a certain way, and one aspect of being feminine is being free – and apparently hair-free!

*   *   *

"You look like a boy!" My mom would often say in Sindhi to me, which indicated she didn't approve of my dress sense. Unflattering clothes, and the need to hide my body, were some of the methods I adopted to shun my femininity. I hid my curves, wore oversized jeans and clogs, refused to wear makeup and preferred a wardrobe of checkered shirts and ties. Dressing like a man didn't just hide my vulnerability, it gave me a swagger and made me feel cool. It also allowed me to hide my hairy body, especially when I found shaving or waxing too much of a chore.

Appearing more masculine was my way of rejecting my burgeoning femininity. I felt a disconnect from my body because it didn't feel safe and left me ashamed to be in it. Shaming myself helped me deal with what had physically happened to me. I blocked and suppressed how I felt as a way to cope but also a way to seem cool and unaffected. My tomboy phase was in high school and some bisexual and lesbian friends began to take an interest in me; flirting with me and actually inviting me out on dates. Chuckling to myself and knowing that I 'didn't swing that way,' I would feel somewhat flattered but rejected their advances.

Validation from my peers gave me the authentication I had been seeking for so long. Masculinity gave me more attention than femininity. My Yang had immense power, and with this newfound role I rejected my Yin more severely, using the attention I was getting to move forward. I wasn't attracted to girls, hence I never took the step to become a lesbian. I had found freedom and happiness by acting and behaving more masculine. Clothes became the primary way to play the part and my behavior definitely gave way to more strength. I had finally found the safe haven I had been searching for all these years. What I noticed later was that courage would be my ultimate guide towards digging deeper into creating a solid balance between the Yin and Yang, as well as remove the mask I was wearing.

In my 20s, tired of feeling unattractive and seeming masculine, I decided to get one of the better-known whitening creams from India called Fairly and Lovely. The advertisements appeared a lot on Star TV so I thought the product had to be good. A great way to trust a product. NOT! I applied a small amount of the white paste onto my face; rubbing the thick mixture around till it smoothed out. I did it a few times, but didn't see how this was going to change my fate. Some can say I didn't have the patience because it does take more than a few attempts for something to work. I had it in my mind that it'll make the change in one or two tries and if it didn't then the product was a failure. An unrealistic standard, perhaps, but it made me see this *flaw* was something that was created by my culture, and I wondered if perhaps my skin color was not inherently bad.

* * *

In 1999, when I worked at Goldman Sachs, grey suits and black heels became my classic uniform. The elevator to the 67th floor of the Cheung Kong Building would give me daily morning jitters as it sped up to the office. It was a huge space with cubicles everywhere. All personnel with different titles were assigned to a cubicle that had our names engraved on a gold plate. When a banker got promoted to a Vice-President position, then he or she was entitled to an office. The office space was painted in mist white with cadet grey carpet and cedar wooden furniture that looked like it was polished daily. Everything was neat and orderly, but it lacked personality and presence. It felt like a cold place even though people would greet and chat with one another. Walking to my desk, I felt like I was on a roller coaster. My stomach would do somersaults for not knowing how my day would unfold. After a while, over the months of my Yang being tested, I got used to the nerves. That wasn't all I got used to. Entering a corporate firm was like being on a new planet. I had to learn countless new tasks – understanding how the intranet works, processing petty cash, answering a phone call and taking notes and at the same time, keeping my eye on the clock for my bosses' conference call dial-in. I learnt how to work at an insane speed and multitask, which were skills I never knew I possessed.

Most of the women who worked there were strong and successful with powerful positions. They reminded me of money-making machines and powerhouses of strength and masculinity. Their personas impressed the insecure part of my psyche, because I felt much lower on the corporate ladder as a mere secretary.

I recall that on one occasion, one of the bankers told me to book her flights and accommodation as she was going to Taipei. Later, she instructed me to have her bag packed, indicating what she wanted. At the time I didn't think packing my boss's bag was part of my job description. My instincts, and my lack of conforming to her demands led to consequences. Upon landing in Taipei, she rang and yelled at me because I apparently forgot to pack a particular top she wanted and was furious at me.

The last time I checked I wasn't hired as 'professional packer' so how was this my problem or wrongdoing? Despite my anger, I didn't say anything and simply apologized.

That day, I had an image of my boss who, though a woman, reminded me of a man. As a matter of fact, she reminded me of a woman cocooned in men's garments. Her rigid suit and stiff-collared shirt pressed with precision with not even one wrinkle made me perceive her as masculine. Calm when she spoke to others below her was hardly evident or rarely present. Her tone emanated determination, aggression, impatience and, paradoxically, charm. In analyzing her from the outside, her behavior didn't exude any of her Yin qualities; femininity, softness, humility and compassion.

Other secretaries in my section probably would have never agreed to pack their banker's suitcase. And it was apparent from the boundaries they placed, which were clear and concise. Some of them seemed to be above me as well. They fundamentally respected themselves and their work ethic. However, I was walked all over, because I didn't know my self-worth. Sensing that the other women were braver than me, desperation to fit in kicked in once again.

At my job, I soon realized that most of the executive women were men in masks, their deportment was ultra-masculine that they too had forgotten who they were. In my opinion, being a feminist does not mean we shun our Yin. My boss was trying to transform herself to fit into a patriarchal world, which absolutely sucked the life out of her Yin. I would never know how she was at home with her family or how she conducted herself around her friends.

Femininity, as I believed, was also about being able to be calm and express without losing one's cool, which was one of the greatest lessons I learnt at Goldman Sachs. Acting 'manly' was the way she chose because it resonated 'toughness' while ensuring that she was seen as 'unbreakable', Every time I encountered her, I wondered if she forgot that she was a person who could express herself calmly.

Part of the beauty of femininity is about learning to be comfortable with vulnerability and that can be in the form of tears or any other emotion. We need to allow ourselves to be okay with how we feel, but not to take it out on others.

Bottling it up like most people do today creates an imbalance and, more often than not we can end up feeling broken, hence affecting the balance between Yin and Yang.

After I was made redundant along with countless other secretaries and bankers, I was unsure what my next steps would be. I had become accustomed to investment banking, and although it paid well, it wasn't a place I felt excited to go to each morning. After some time, I landed a teaching assistant job, which was very different from my previous role but I was willing to give it a try. I was 28, and making less than half of what I had earned previously. I never thought my life would change so drastically – being in an elementary school environment was worlds apart from being in the corporate realm. In this atmosphere, I saw passion, compassion, integrity and humility. People were genuinely friendly and caring towards one another. As green as I was in the field of education without university qualifications, I was never made to feel inferior or inadequate, but instead I felt welcomed and a part of the community. As a TA, I was guided by teachers on what my role and responsibilities were and I was encouraged to shadow other TAs and teachers so I had a range of skill sets and ideas to learn from.

I had a mentor, Rama, who took me under her wing. She was a senior teacher who taught science to middle-school students. Rama was approachable, had a lot of advice and wisdom to impart, and she became someone I could turn to. After being there for nearly a year, I was encouraged by her and the Head of School to consider going back to school to get a Bachelor in Education, since I had discovered that I was passionate about children and teaching. Opening that door was a turning point in my life.

The process of applying to a university was arduous because I couldn't afford to go to university on my own. Luckily, I was able to get a grant from the government, which reduced the financial burden. The other difficult part of being an undergraduate student at 28, was that I was going against a cultural and family norm of studying at a later stage in my life, which was unheard of a decade ago. I never thought it would happen even though obtaining a degree had always been one of the most important goals I wanted to achieve in my life. I felt having a degree would mean I was able to earn a decent living, which in today's society gives you more power. In an Indian household, boys are expected and encouraged to get higher education because they are the sole breadwinners, while girls are trained to be homemakers. There is a huge divide in gender equality, especially among Indians. Having the opportunity to potentially change the course of my life was what drove me forward. It wasn't just power I was seeking, but also wanting to feel like an equal and as an Indian girl that couldn't have been more important. My life had already been controlled by many other people and circumstances and I wasn't living the life I chose. As an undergraduate student at 28, this was my first attempt at taking a stand to live my life on my own terms. I felt like the lotus flower emerging from the murky water.

While I was studying and changing my future, my understanding of boundaries was a blur. Being a lady also meant knowing whether I was being treated like one. It doesn't mean having the princess syndrome or being a brat. To me it means knowing my boundaries and what I am willing to accept and what I'm not as a woman. I do not accept being spoken down to just because I am a woman, although I have certainly experienced it. I didn't understand this yet when I was dating and didn't yet know my self-worth, and I accepted being used or manipulated by guys. In my third year of university, I was dating a guy, Navin, who treated me like his ATM machine. He had excessive excuses for not ever having money. He would constantly order more beer and then whisky whenever we were out. His behavior was worrying for me because I was studying and working, too. Even though I was counting my pennies I was allowing his behavior. I had no one to blame but myself. Where was my voice and why wasn't I using it? The fear of not being wanted was far greater than wanting to be treated well.

As a woman trying to live my own life, I need to be treated as an equal because the opportunity to pursue my dreams puts me, a girl, on the same footing as a man. Femininity means to embrace grace, calm, integrity and sensuality, and it's important to know that these qualities are no less valuable than masculine ones.

Adjusting to student life, learning how to write essays, adapting to my peers who were younger, and ensuring I did well in order to get a decent job; put extreme pressure on me. I turned to my maturity and desire for the reasons I wanted to obtain a degree. My passion drove me to the finish line. When I stood on the stage, wearing my black gown, receiving my Bachelor of Education certificate in English Language and graduating with a 2.1, I knew something had transformed in me. When my brother started tearing, shocked at the fact I had managed to do it despite the challenges, it gave him a glimpse of my determination. It was a proud moment to be there with my peers, brother, Mama and my friend Cara by my side. I knew my life was about to change.

When girls are given an opportunity to study and work, it allows them to be who they want to be, and that in itself is not just liberating but empowering.

In my 30s, a lot shifted. I now had an undergraduate degree, and landed a great teaching job, which paid well. I was able to pay for the exorbitant cost of lasering my body. Yes, I said body. Laser is, believe it or not, excruciatingly painful. It must have been the excessive hair and the ingrown hairs under my skin from shaving that made it torturous. It was like being poked with needles on each follicle. Not to mention, the salon looked more like a hospital because everything was white and the very friendly therapists wore nurse uniforms, which only amplified the hospital ambiance. I was escorted to an ice-cold, sterile treatment room. Before the process of lasering starts, you're iced to numb the area that is being lasered. I detest being cold, so that was a twofold blow. The process of laser hair removal made me cry. Tears would run down my cheeks even though I knew that there was an end to it. Eventually I would forever be hair free, from the years of suffering the pain of full-body hair removal. And today, I am free. It allowed my skin to glow while still being dark. The reflection in the mirror astonished me, "Wow, I am pretty!" I remember saying to myself. This was when my journey towards understanding my own ideas of beauty began.

Externally I felt feminine and was proud to run my hands across my now smooth skin. At times, I would stare at my own skin, surprised at the changes it had undergone. While my skin transformed, my body needed a bit of work especially when hitting 30. The way I looked had changed and I had never exercised other than the PE lessons I had in high school. I joined a gym, and after shedding a few kilos I was pleased with my slimmer look. Soon I got introduced to kickboxing by one of the instructors in my gym.

The addiction came on quickly! I certainly wasn't well-coordinated initially, but the punches and kicks made me feel like I was releasing a lot of pent-up emotions. Wanting to explore this area more, I decided to join an MMA gym, Impakt, which was founded by Alain Ngalani, the World Champion in kickboxing. When I stepped off the escalator to the second floor, I was swarmed by testosterone. The bright red reception area was like my buffer zone, allowing me to calm my nerves for what awaited beyond that area. A sweet lady at the front desk greeted me, asked me some basic fitness questions and gave me a tour of the gym. I saw naked, sweaty men. Their muscles carved out like Greek Gods. I was thinking, "I am definitely in the wrong place. What is a petite girl like myself doing in a male-dominated gym?" (Though I am five feet five inches tall, in front of many six-foot muscular men, I felt tiny like a snail!) I could hear grunts that were as loud as thunder. The beefed-up men walking around looking like the Hulk petrified me. I felt so out of place.

It was in December during a lunchtime session, so there weren't many people around, which eased my nerves slightly. It was like my first day in school where everyone was gorgeous and fit and I looked like an ugly duckling. I signed up for a trial class and to my surprise I didn't feel out of place and I enjoyed it! We were punching bags, kicking and doing all sorts of combinations. My left kick was appalling, but the trainer seemed impressed and that boosted my confidence. It felt like school over again. When a teacher is pleased with you, it boosts you to work harder and this had the same effect. After a while, I decided to sign up and got private sessions, and joined group classes. Muay Thai was my favorite sport because I had an avenue to channel all my pent-up pain, which I wasn't able to express verbally. It was the perfect outlet and fantastically therapeutic.

Months later, Alain became my trainer and it was brutal because he expected the world out of his clients. You don't just train, you train beyond your limit, which I loved. I learnt so much about myself after two years of being a member at Impakt. I got comfortable being around good-looking men who were also compassionate and kind to their female partners. It was a learning curve because I had a belief system that men were assholes. Who could blame me after being abused by someone I was supposed to trust and was living in the same house as me? The experience at Impakt changed how I viewed men and I no longer categorized men as pricks who would always let me down or fail me. I started to be more open about men in general and it made dating easier while becoming more ladylike. Gone were the days of me dressing like a man – the lady was out and the beast stayed in the Muay Thai ring.

Usually I would leave the gym in my gym gear, and just go home. But on one occasion, I was going out for a meal so I had to shower and put on something other than my gym gear. What happened after that incident has had a lasting impact on me. That day, after I finished training, I showered and got dressed. I left the changing room with a short tight black dress, stilettos and some make up. I got 'wows' from the trainers. Initially I thought there was someone behind me, because "it couldn't be me?" I thought to myself. Soon after, I realized it was *me* they were looking at. I blushed and was lost for words. I acted cool and continued walking out to the reception area. Their reaction made me feel like I had somehow made it. It wasn't because they complimented me about my physical appearance. People noticed me as a 'lady', and in that moment, I felt feminine.

I knew I was changing but when you get an off-the-cuff compliment, it does feel good! While I was blushing inside, I realized that I was getting the right balance of femininity without looking slutty. I wasn't fundamentally seeking validation from a guy – it could have been a girl saying that I looked stunning. It simply meant, in my mind, "I have what it takes to turn heads," and it felt liberating for me to know I had that hidden in me somewhere .

In my late-30s, I began learning to Tango. It seemed to have just fallen into my life, though I had always been a big fan of dancing. As a kid, I used to do *Bharatnatyam*, which is classical Indian dance. I loved wearing Indian outfits because of their colors and embroidery. But more importantly, I was connected to the moves, which exuded honor and grace. The instructor would explain the words to the song we were learning and it was enchanting. I was always swept away by how the movements had meaning and a story. The Bharatnatyam was a way to honor Krishna or other Hindu deities, and it felt like devotion in action.

My husband and I had our first private Tango lesson together, which brought out my inner self. It was similar to meditation, in the sense that I felt like an observer of my mind while simultaneously letting go. With Tango, you let go and let the man lead you. As a woman, you trust your partner and you naturally flow with the movements. The feeling of floating was like a butterfly flying while showing its beauty to the world. I felt that was what a man should do – lead the woman through the dance, while showing off her beauty to the world, through trust and letting go. It was a complete and absolute surrender of the body, mind and senses. It was a beautiful meditative experience of connecting with my husband, but also learning how to touch into the softness in me. The ability to dance as if I am flowing like water flows in the river was no doubt one of the most magical experiences I have had in my life. Tango gave the Yin back to my Yang.

As Tango became an integral part of my life, wearing dresses made even more sense. Heels and dresses were normal attire, so I purchased a pair of tango stilettos and continued my journey of femininity through the art of dance. As my clothing changed, my body and my stance began to reform itself as well. I felt like a woman, and that affected how I walked, sat and carried myself. I observed myself and consciously evolved.

It was through looking at my unspoken beliefs – such as that I didn't deserve an education because of my gender, or that I wasn't beautiful because of my complexion and reflecting on the ugly truth of my past – that has catalyzed the shift in me towards becoming more feminine. Rejecting my feminine side was a protection mechanism, and was also due to not feeling good enough about myself. While I wanted to embrace my Yin, I also didn't believe I deserved it because I was embarrassed and didn't like myself. I rejected my Yin and it spilled into every aspect of my life. Letting my Yang dominate me resulted in countless failed romantic relationships. Not standing up for what I wanted – such as going back to school and not knowing how to embrace my body and be proud of being a girl – were things I slowly learnt about myself.

Femininity is the essence of every woman; it is our true nature. It is like telling Buddha not to be an enlightened being. I was rejecting my core self because I was ashamed and when that was recognized, the layers came back on slowly and gradually. My truth and reality was to embrace who I am; a woman who loves her body despite its flaws, understands my body and its needs, respects the needs of what I desire, and strives to be treated as an equal. This world needs both men and women to be comfortable about being themselves whatever that may be, while still making an impact on others. I was on that journey to discover what it means to be feminine, extrinsically and intrinsically.

The more I got in touch with my feminine side, the more I realized who my grandma epitomized. My grandma was not just a perfectionist, but also a fashionista. She liked getting her nails done, wearing makeup and it would usually be red lipstick and red manicured fingers and toes. She loved colors and her clothes matched her hair accessories, and her handbag matched her sandals. She took her time and pride in looking immaculate, which I now admire. Besides being glamorous, even though she wasn't educated, she was respected. She knew her boundaries and no one would challenge her or dare speak to her disrespectfully. She had a great balance of the Yin and the Yang. She was feminine and also very comfortable being masculine by saying what she felt even if someone took offense. As I was diving into rediscovering myself, I realized what I consider to be feminine aligns with Big Mama's philosophy.

She was a role model because of how she integrated the internal and external aspects of femininity. Each day I aspire to be more like her; graceful and confident in her value as a woman.

The Pressure To Conform

"Whenever you find yourself on the side of the majority, it's time to pause and reflect."

— Mark Twain

I had experienced being bullied in elementary school and it boiled down to my complexion so whilst I couldn't change that, I made sure I would fit in in other aspects of high school. I went to an American high school and because it was a private school, many of my schoolmates came from wealthy families so it was the norm to have the latest trendy apparel and school things. While I came from a middle-class family, my parents certainly did not revel in spending money on materialistic things for both my brother and myself. I remember telling my father how I wanted a specific bag for school but after taking me to the store, he refused, remarking that it was too expensive for just a schoolbag. I was so upset and it made me feel like he didn't care. It wasn't just a bag to me. Back then, fitting in was my core mission at school, and since I had already been bullied, my burning desire to fit in with school fashion was an attempt to make up for my insecurities.

This was the beginning of my father's control over how my journey in life would pan out. Being controlled was suffocating and I felt trapped but there were times I felt like a regular kid with a 'normal' family going out for meals to my favorite Korean restaurant. Dad was strict and yet there were times he was reasonable. I had curfews like most teenagers – I was able to go out at night or to a friend's place and have friends stay over. I vacationed in Japan and Jakarta to see relatives. It was easier for me to paint a picture of him being an awful father who gave me nothing but pain. He caused me suffering, but my attempt at sweeping his actions under the carpet was to try to live a 'normal' life. I had a private education and completed high school even if it meant I had to beg to complete Grade 12 and graduate. Completing high school did change the course of my life because a decade later, it enabled me to go to university. Nevertheless, for decades, there were a series of trivial as well as major incidents that made life seem impossible.

If my parents had known about my turmoil at school, I wonder if that would have changed their view of me craving to have the bloody school bag! And if my dad gave me the bag, he would have somehow admitted to knowing that I so desperately needed to fit in. My desire to belong was becoming unattainable and I believed this bag could save me.

Most of the girls in my clique seemed to be wealthy and of a certain elite group. Dr. Martens shoes and clothes from Benetton and Esprit were the standard. Luckily we had uniforms, but once a month we had 'free dress day' at school but only if we didn't get caught speaking a language other than English. Imagine the humiliation of going to school on a free dress day when all your friends are dressed in casuals and you're the odd one out wearing a uniform. Even though English is my first language, I got caught a few times speaking Cantonese. Each time a student got caught, they had to pay 10 dollars or do 10 push-ups. Being fluent in a few languages, and then getting punished for speaking them by having to wear school uniform on a casual dress day made me stand out like a sore thumb, which was exactly what I didn't want. Besides, I was in Hong Kong, and speaking Cantonese made me feel like I fit into society. Having a steadfast black-and-white rule regarding language doesn't work.

Sharon learnt that I wanted a bag that my father refused to buy. She took me to the shop, asked me which one I wanted and just like that, she bought it for me. Entering the shop, I felt like a three-year-old entering a candy store. I was over the moon being in the store, and then leaving with a newly purchased bag in my hand! I was amazed at how she did it. I knew the money was my father's, but she was able to override him. Clearly, he wasn't the one in charge like he portrayed. I saw the power she had over him, and it definitely taught me about manipulation and how dating works. This was just the beginning of what I discovered about her.

After spending more time with her, I wondered why she bought me the bag. I wasn't her daughter, so there was no reason for her to be overly generous. Besides, she had a daughter of her own with him so there was no need for her to go out of her way with me. What I suspect was that she knew my father was close to me so she felt she had to win me over and this was a perfect way to get her foot in the 'emotional' door, and it worked. While I knew she was the 'other woman' I was still desperate for maternal love. My mom was closer to my brother than me, so any kind of love was love. Sharon could sense the strained relationship I had with my mom and Sharon used that to her advantage.

Once, I was over at the guesthouse at which she stayed when Sharon visited Hong Kong with her daughter. She was giving her daughter a bath. I observed enviously because I didn't remember a time when my mother had done that, besides knowing, as an infant, my mom gave me the painful body scrubs. Sharon gestured me to get into the bathtub. I was shy, but with a little convincing, I got in and it felt so good to feel like someone was taking care of me. In that moment, I was in the presence of a mother-like figure and even though she was in no way a mom to me, she made the effort and gave me the attention I needed to make me feel loved.

As a teenager, it was so confusing to figure out what was going on with the adult relationships around me. I trusted what my father told me. Especially the negative things about my mom, which made it seem like she was in the wrong hence justifying why he was having an affair. But what he did caused a rift between my mom and myself, because I believed the things he said about her; like that she wasn't tender with my dad like a wife should be. I could feel that there was tension in the air of who was in the wrong and whose side we (my brother and I) were on.

Today, when I reflect, I can see that this was so twisted for so many reasons. Parents shouldn't take sides and they shouldn't involve their kids in their marital issues. It causes so much stress and discomfort for the children. While I have no kids of my own, having seen what they did definitely has taught me how to be around children and how to ensure that they feel loved regardless of what the adults in their presence are going through. Perhaps my parents didn't know any better because they married so young or because it was an arranged marriage. All a child needs is to be loved and whoever shows affection will attract the child to them. Hence I gravitated towards my father and being close to him meant I was having to see his mistress and daughter, too.

I was overjoyed that I finally had the bag of my dreams. It felt like I could finally be like everyone else. Somehow this bag meant so much to me that when I got it, I used it for years unlike most of my friends, who changed their accessories with the seasons. I knew how much I wanted it and for this reason I wasn't going to change bags all the time like the others. Having it was a symbol of feeling like I finally belonged.

There was so much going on in high school, and things were always busy. I was a rebellious kid on occasion, depending on the teacher and the subject. I never liked anything related to math or science. When I had to sit through those subjects, I'd switch off. Since I can remember, math made no logical sense to me, even if it is the most logical of the subjects. I couldn't fathom why we had to learn trigonometry or calculus. I didn't comprehend any of the formulas or why there were alphabets thrown in and then a number would be the result. It was like an alien language to me.

Today I am fascinated by physics and chemistry as I see the relevance they have to energy and the latter to food and how it is produced and the chemical balance we need in our bodies. None of that was taught in my school. It seemed that most of what I learnt at school wasn't relevant to real-life skills. Or maybe I didn't have the maturity to understand the relevance like I do today. Math was harder. I had a teacher, Mr. Dubois, who taught me both french and math, so that was tough. Tough because for french I would earn an A or B, which made it easier for him to be fond of me. But then when I had math, because I was awful in it, I would be terrified. He transformed from being a pleasant teacher in french to a scary monster-like teacher in math. He would randomly pick on students to go to the blackboard to figure out an equation, which meant I'd get embarrassed in front of the whole class when I couldn't do it.

One day in Grade 9, my best friend Amy and I were called to the blackboard during our algebra class. I vividly remember the classroom had taupe desks and chairs and white fluorescent lights. He wrote an equation on the blackboard, and even though his handwriting was beautiful to look at, what he wrote puzzled us. He stood at the back of the room and saw how we tried to formulate an answer. It felt like judgment day. If we met his expectation, which was to get it right, he would like us but if we didn't then he wouldn't. Luckily, I had taken some tutorial classes after school so I wasn't that bad because I could at least write down some of the steps to the equation even though I was still struggling, but Amy was out of her depth. I remember everyone's eyes were fixated on us. Time had stopped and we were standing there, figuring out this equation. It reminded us of our days in primary school because we'd constantly get picked on in math class and at times, we'd end up giggling. They were the kind of giggles that you can't stop and you have no idea why exactly you're laughing. We had those especially at the wrong times and it made the teachers furious. After what felt like hours, we went back to our seats, and he went to the board to mark our answer.

Mr. Dubois had a fatherly look to him; he was stern, with high expectations, neat handwriting, smelled nice and he loved his coffee. In many ways, he reminded me of my own father. My father had beautiful handwriting, loved his cologne and paid close attention to details. His face was buried in a bushy beard and it was often hard to anticipate what he was thinking. He had big brown piercing eyes that wore no smile, which made him look harsh and came across as intimidating. I badly wanted his approval.

Chemistry was another story. In Grade 10, I had Mr. Tei and it seemed that he didn't have his heart in the right place as a teacher, or looking at it from his perspective, it could have been that we were impossible to teach. We were a rowdy class; we were loud, had too much energy and at times were just plain obnoxious. We were at the stage where we probably thought we were adults so we felt entitled to do as we pleased, and we did. Our corner classroom felt spacious, with the typical taupe desks and chairs and fluorescent lights. If we weren't entertained, or if the teacher didn't know how to be a mixture of fun and firm, we switched off. It took a special kind of teacher to get through to us. We would consistently talk amongst ourselves and were easily bored. Some of us would play games or pass notes to each other. Others would even sleep and you could sometimes hear the low hum of snoring whilst the lesson was progressing through its stages. During Mr. Tei's lessons, I'd do my trigonometry homework because I knew if I didn't, I'd get hell from Mr. Dubois. We weren't scared of Mr. Tei, partially because he didn't get mad or lose it like Mr. Dubois. It came across like he couldn't be bothered. Eventually, Mr. Tei had a chat, like teachers do, with my homeroom teacher, Ms. Dobbs.

Ms. Dobbs reminded me of a young hippie type of teacher from New York. She was fashionable with blonde hair and had great style. Some of my friends and I were really fond of her because she looked so cool. One day, after art class, she asked me to stay behind. I was worried, but didn't think too much of it. She told me what Mr. Tei said, that I wasn't behaving in class and that I was making it hard for him to teach. I started crying. The fact that he told Ms. Dobbs meant he did care. Ms. Dobbs wasn't angry or upset with me, she just wanted to know if something was going on that was making it hard for me to concentrate. The care I felt from Ms. Dobbs changed not just how I saw myself as a student, but also the inner workings and dynamics of my home and family life. I trusted her implicitly. Finally, for the first time, I admitted something was not right. I told her about my father and what he was doing to me. It felt like I was in a movie about my own life. I saw tears rolling down her cheeks, and her reaction made me realize how serious this was. In a panic, she said, "Come and stay with me!" I think what I was going through hurt her deeply. She was hoping she could make a difference and that she could make it stop by convincing my father during the next parents' day that I ought to go to university in the United States.

Ms. Dobbs could see that what my father was doing to me was making me insecure in class, and all aspects of my life. She wanted nothing more for me than to be free from him. At parents' day, he agreed to let me go to university in the States, or that was what my father said to her, and I innocently believed him. When I got home, he revealed to me that he appeased my teacher Ms. Dobbs by saying all the things she wanted to hear about university so she would mind her own business. He didn't want to have that conversation with her, about what he was doing to me or what he had been doing to me since I was five – so he lied and led her to believe that he was going to send me to the US to further my studies.

When I found out that my father had lied to Ms. Dobbs, I was devastated because all of my friends applied to universities. Once again I was left out, different from my peers, and my parents – especially my father – couldn't or refused to see it. I was told that my destiny as an Indian girl was to get married. There was no need for me to go to university because I'd be married off anyway. It didn't matter that I, personally, didn't want to get married.

When I told Ms. Dobbs that I wasn't going to go to university she was upset, but she also knew that there was nothing she could do. Back then, we had no computers at home as this was the early 90s, and soon after graduation, we lost touch.

During the summer break, Ms. Dobbs was around for the holidays so she invited me, and my friend, Susan, over for dinner. We felt privileged to be in her house and to talk to her about our personal problems and to get to know her as a person. I felt so close to her. I felt I had a big sister I could turn to and who was there for me. I was sad because she was leaving Hong Kong after the holidays.

Losing her was hard but like with everything in life, when one door closes another one opens. I was in Málaga, Spain, one summer holiday visiting my grandparents and I met a girl, Roma, who was five years older. The weird thing was she lived in Hong Kong, but I barely spoke to her because I was shy and she looked too cool and popular to talk to. I distinctly remember her long curly hair and that she was wearing short denim shorts and lots of jewelry when we first met. Because her parents and my grandparents were close friends, I had a chance to hang out with her in Málaga. We went to the beach and walked around the town center. I remember looking at her and wanting to be like her. When I was back in Hong Kong, we remained close and she easily became a sister and that was very comforting. I used to write poems and fax them to her brother's office and at times, I'd write her letters and give them to her when I saw her. I had all this pent-up love that I poured out to her. She reciprocated, which filled my empty heart.

Roma was there for me and never stopped giving me advice whether it was about dating, going back to university, or the conflicts I had with people around me. She was the sounding board I needed when I was confused or made wrong decisions.

At 19, I applied to a writing school in Singapore using the supplementary credit card that my dad had given me for my 18th birthday. I didn't tell him and I wasn't supposed to use the credit card for big purchases, but I was desperate to study. My love for writing pushed me to apply even though I knew it went against my father's wishes and I hadn't asked for permission. When the course materials arrived, he was livid and yelled at me. He rang the school and explained how he never agreed for me to study and he wanted a refund. I was crushed and petrified that being in complete control of me, my father would never allow me to move forward.

In hindsight, I often wonder if something atrocious took place in my father's own life for him to act the way he did. I feel incredibly sorry for him and in my opinion it makes my heart more open to the notion that he might have been in a dangerous situation when he was younger, so that's why he was acting out in his later years. The one thing I realized is that his need for me to conform was so that he could control me. And this has taught me to let things go, because controlling the past is not something we can do. It's gone. Finished. Part of a distant memory, which doesn't need focus or attention. A grand lesson for me to move forward.

*　　*　　*

After being made redundant at my position as a secretary in an investment bank, I applied for a number of different jobs. I was granted an interview for a teaching assistant position at Carmel School, a private Jewish school that follows the American curriculum and teaches Hebrew and Jewish studies. I had no clue that this job would be the turning point in my life. I worked as a TA for Grade 1 and the kids were so adorable. Their innocence made me think of my own childhood and how my father never helped me preserve that.

I observed the teachers with fervor as a TA. I worked over the summer so I could get paid, learn more about the school and expand my skills. I worked in the school office and acted as the Head of School's personal assistant. The year started and I was assigned to the same kids, so I moved up with them. By then, we had established a good rapport. I started to find my place in the school. I had some wonderful mentors who guided and taught me about the curriculum and even though I was a TA, they respected me. It was then that the Principal and Head of School suggested that I go back to university. They asked me to do a demo lesson and I remember that, after completing the lesson plan for it, I was so nervous that I couldn't sleep the night before. It was after the demo lesson that they felt I was a natural and that it would be a waste of my skills if I continued as a TA. I was scared, but so flattered. It was then that the topic of university came back into my life, a decade later.

At 28 my life was difficult because I was doing something that wasn't ordinary or appreciated. According to my community, I was expected to get married. Being a student at my age created a plethora of gossip. I was supposed to bring in money and not spend money; all these rules I was up against didn't make my decision easy, but then again my life from the start had never been smooth sailing so I continued to take the path less travelled.

Adjusting to university life was hard especially the first year, but by the time the second year rolled in, I got the hang of things and did fairly well. I probably was one of the rare Sindhi girls in Hong Kong who went up against family and social expectations to attend university at that age. Some did, but usually after marriage, because they were trying to find their career path or interest. For some families, going to university was more acceptable but for some reason it wasn't accepted in mine. I guess the fear was that if I was too educated then I'd be smarter than the guy I would marry and, to them, that never looks good. I was constantly told that no guy wants a woman who's smarter than him.

I graduated, landed a great teaching job and devoted myself to it. I was 32 and single, so doing well in my first 'real' job meant the world to me. I gave it my all. I am still in touch with my former students, especially those I trained in debating.

A few years ago, I spent months trying to find Ms. Dobbs when it was fairly easy to reconnect with anyone thanks to Facebook – I had no luck in locating her. On Facebook, we have a group for our class (class of 93) and one of my classmates, Patrick, got in touch with me, remembering how close I was to Ms. Dobbs.

He told me that she had changed her name from Gillian Dobbs to Shakti Sutriasa and Patrick found her website. I was so happy and I couldn't believe it! I felt like I was back in Grade 12 again! I was so excited at the possibility of reconnecting with her. I sent Ms. Dobbs an email and I didn't think she'd reply because it had been over two decades and she could have forgotten me. When I got her email in response, I was over the moon! We caught up a bit over email and scheduled to have a Skype session. When we Skyped, we cried so much. I felt like I had gone back in time. We had picked up where we left off and yet we had grown so much. She was someone who inspired me and believed in me, and I felt that her supportive voice was always inside my head.

And again, four years later we had another catch-up and I realized something I hadn't known. We have similar career experiences. She was a high school teacher turned counselor and writer. I am all three. I don't fit in a box. I have tried to assimilate, only to realize I can't. I am not meant to be like everyone else; I am meant to stand out because I believe I am different. I have a story that is unusual. I knew as a child that I would become a writer one day and make a difference to children. And Ms. Dobbs was definitely the first person who planted the seed of writing in me and coaxed me gently to pursue writing my memoir. My current goal, especially with where I stand today, is to help girls understand the rules around boundaries, consent and permission.

Today, I'm in my 40s and obtained two Master's degrees after my undergraduate studies. The painful fact that my dreams had been trampled on by someone I cared about was part of the reason I wanted to excel, and prove him wrong, as well as everyone else in my community. Just because I had been raped, and lived in silence for so long, it was not going to hinder me from fulfilling my dreams and pursuing my passions. The tools I have learnt through teaching have given me insight into how our youth handle themselves during times of crisis, as well as monumental positive milestones like getting accepted to university, and through the mirror of their experiences I have had the chance to reflect deeply upon my own.

Dating

"Before we can have a successful relationship with anyone, we first need a perfect personal relationship."

— **Russ Von Hoelscher**

I dated quite a few different types of men from my early 20s onwards, until I finally met the man I would marry. Many members of my family were confused as to why I *wouldn't* settle down. I kept getting the fortnightly question, "When are you finally going to get married and settle down?" When it came down to it, marriage wasn't on my wide spectrum of priorities at that time in my life. Maybe it was because I was attracted to all sorts of men that weren't ever really right for me, and something within me knew that. There were a few men who were perfect for me – they were kind, respectful and lived by a good moral code. I found myself attracted to them initially and things seemed to be heading in the right direction. But I eventually discovered that those qualities were not enough and I let them go. I think deep down that this was due to my own insecurities, but at the time I told myself that there was something missing. When I reflect on those times I can't help thinking that I made mistakes. Good guys never seemed like they were enough and always seemed to slip through the net.

I repeatedly found myself in relationships with men who were totally wrong for me. These guys often made me feel lousy about myself and as the relationships progressed these feelings only got worse. I ended up giving too much of myself in order to secure these relationships, which inevitably resulted in them taking more of a step back!

There were also a variety of men I dated that were just different versions of my father, which wasn't something I was proud of. I instinctively knew that men who were like my father were wrong for me, yet I found myself falling over and over again for their charm and sophistication. Before I knew it, I was blinded by love. It was as if some of these guys had the ability to put a love spell on me! Anyone from the outside could see I wasn't in a healthy relationship, but I was continuously unable to see clearly. Nothing could make me see the truth, often until it was too late.

So what's really wrong with being with someone who's like my father? For most girls there would be nothing wrong with dating someone who has similar characteristics and values to their father. Many girls regard their father as a perfect benchmark of what to look for in a partner. But sadly my father was not a good benchmark. He was a complicated man. He got married at the age of 20 to my mom, whom he had never met until their wedding day. He never really had the chance to date other women prior to marrying my mom. He was always under the watchful eye of his parents until that point. After getting married, he resorted to having affairs in abundance. These continued unabated for many years. His sexual desire was over the top and he didn't know how to control it.

My father had an enormous impact on how I interacted with men. My father was a charmer and considered a ladies' man. He had a way with words, especially with women. As a result, I dated men who were smooth talkers and knew when to say the right thing to win me over. They left me weak in the knees even after saying something to put me down. It was classic manipulation hidden behind charm.

I was clueless of how dating worked and how the 'game' was meant to be played. Men who play this game mask it so well that some women are unable to realize that they are being played. Guys who behave in this way are experts at knowing how to manipulate a woman's psyche. I was constantly drawn back in like a yo-yo with no idea as to why I had even returned. Quite often after I went back to a person, I found myself being given the cold shoulder. I would find myself feeling insecure and eventually would skulk back. Dating was like learning a complicated, emotionally dangerous new skill. I needed a set of instructions that I was never given. In my opinion, there are only a lucky few who appear to have this instruction manual, and they seem to have made a secret promise with each other to not share it with anyone else. If it was shared, there would be a few less broken hearts.

As an Indian, I tried really hard to please my family but had limited success. Being the only daughter in the family came with the huge pressure of marrying a guy the family would approve of. Their high standards dictated that the guy I married had to be of the same ethnicity – Sindhi. The standards also required that the guy should come from a good family, have a decent career, and have strong moral values. India would be the ideal place where I could find men who matched these values. When India didn't work out, I tried to find the right guy on my own. I believed it was important to be the best daughter I could be, which meant marrying someone who would fit in well with my family and its traditions and values. In Indian culture, a woman isn't just marrying the man, she is also marrying the entire family. Some couples are expected to live with the guy's parents, so knowing that the family is reputable helps ease the bride into a new family. I tried finding my own Indian prince after I realized I wanted to be like everyone else. I longed to be a normal Indian girl, and to make my family proud. My challenge was that I was very attracted to men who weren't Indian. Eventually, I went with my gut instinct and tried dating non-Indians.

Jon was my first non-Indian guy I was emotionally involved with. He was a six foot seven, Swedish, blonde-haired, sparkly blue-eyed guy who resembled a Viking warrior from mythological times. He was a sweet, caring and sociable guy who was generally friendly towards everyone he met. His outgoing personality came with his job. He ran a bar in Macau and that was how we initially met. My family and I would have regular weekend getaways in Macau. Occasionally, we'd stay at the hotel where Jon worked. My brother and I would enjoy a few drinks and end up partying at the bar till late. I never spoke to Jon much. I was a bit reserved and shy, which wasn't abnormal behavior for me at this stage in my life. He didn't say a lot either. On one occasion Jon gave me his business card. I didn't think much of it. Sometime later, I sent him an email and that was how it all started. As the courtship progressed, feelings developed. But nothing really came out of it. We weren't able to meet up often because of his work schedule and my university studies. The relationship dragged on and when he prioritized trips elsewhere over seeing me, I got upset. I felt that his actions were showing how little I meant to him.

I later discovered that Jon didn't want to step on my brother's toes because dating me meant having to deal with my brother. My brother was conventional when it came to who I dated, as I was his little sister. My brother is a year-and-a-half older than me and we have a special bond. Because I mean so much to him, he didn't think anyone who showed any interest was good enough for me. Ever since our father left in 1998, my brother has tried his best to be like a father figure to me. One of the typical roles of a father is to approve – or not – who your daughter dates and those were the shoes he was filling for me.

I know my brother cared deeply for me. While this was endearing, it was also difficult to talk to him about a guy that I fancied. My brother had the opinion that men in general were players. In order to be with me, they needed to step up and show me that they were for real. When I was younger, I didn't understand any of this. I thought he was being overly strict and patriarchal.

It is not the norm in Indian society for a girl to stay over at a guy's place. Jon probably knew this and it would have been a very tough relationship for him to handle. Ten years ago, I saw him in Singapore. I was staying at a hotel and my friends and I went for drinks at the hotel bar where he so happened to be working. Before I knew it, he was standing inches away from me. He was so excited to see me that he came straight over and lifted me way up into the air. I felt we had picked up where we had left off. But I was sadly mistaken.

Jon and I had a friend in common called Cassidy, who mentioned a couple of days later that he had changed. He told me, "He isn't the guy you knew before. He's not good for you."

I had no idea what that meant and it confused me. I met Jon for lunch the day I was leaving because I wanted to find out what Cassidy was talking about. Jon explained what Cassidy was trying to warn me about. I could see that Jon was distant and there was nothing between us. I realized then that Cassidy was right; he was not interested in a romantic long-term relationship with me at all. I misjudged his reaction when he saw me and lifted me up. I assumed he wanted to be with me because he seemed excited to see me. Maybe a part of him did, but the bigger part of him had changed. Hence Cassidy advised me that he wasn't good for me. Being with me would be too much of an effort for him. After all, he was surrounded by all kinds of different women in the bar who would regularly throw themselves at him. Maybe one night stands and flings were where he was at at this stage in his life. He wasn't ready to be with one woman.

I was disappointed because of how we had reconnected at the bar. His reaction convinced me that he felt the same way. I couldn't comprehend the fact that he had changed over time. I felt cheated, like I was being made a fool of. One moment he was hot and then the next he was ice-cold. How can a girl ever trust that a guy is consistent if their feelings or behavior change as quickly as the Hong Kong weather?

I returned to Hong Kong and was feeling low, worse than when I had left. I made the classic mistake of texting to try to win him back. I know now that if a guy wants a girl, he will do what it takes to be with her. It is as simple as that. My pride and self-esteem had dissolved because I let myself fall so deeply for someone. I felt that I could convince him that we were good for each other. When I couldn't get him back, it reinforced a belief I had about myself that I wasn't good enough. If I was, I told myself, he'd be with me. I realized that seeking validation from him was my downfall. I was desperate for love because I never felt that I had ever been truly loved before.

*   *   *

In my mid-20s, I met someone online. At first it seemed to flow naturally and I was quite excited about the relationship. The most positive thing about it was that he was Indian. His name was Anil. He was of the same ethnicity. He was of average build and height with a small dark goatee. He was a successful entrepreneur who lived in London. At first glance, he seemed to have lovely parents, who cared a lot about him. If I had had a checklist, he would have ticked all the boxes. At that time, technology hadn't advanced to the point of having video chat like Skype. So I based what I thought he looked like from the pictures he sent. After months of getting to know him through phone calls and texts, he said we should finally meet. If the meeting went well, we could get engaged. I felt as if I was on cloud nine. My logical, critical brain disappeared and went on a holiday. I didn't stop to think or evaluate the situation properly. The truth of the matter was I felt wanted, and that was a huge relief.

He convinced me to go to London to see him. Logically, it made no sense because I wasn't doing well financially. But I jumped on a plane. I also had to persuade my mom to come along, which was a difficult venture. He assured me that if she came and we hit it off, we would get engaged. I was flattered at how much he had thought about me and our relationship, albeit long distance. I didn't see any red flags. Most guys would take their time and be in a relationship before talking about proposing. But in this case, I trusted the process I was getting into.

My plan worked and we set off to London. My brother wasn't pleased about the whole situation. He didn't see why we had to fly over to see Anil and not the other way around. In his mind, if the guy is interested, he makes the first move. That is how it should work in our community, which I totally understand now. In my naïveté, I felt I had to jump on it or I'd lose him. With my mom by my side, I felt like this was my chance in securing a future with a guy.

We arrived in London and, from the very beginning it felt fundamentally wrong. Initially, I was confused that it was even him. He didn't resemble the photo he sent and I simply didn't recognize him. The photo was probably taken a decade ago and he had aged and gained a great deal of weight. This was in sharp contrast to the photos he recently sent. He didn't greet us with any real etiquette at the airport. Anil was cold and distant with my mom and relatives who had come to pick us up. He acted like he was superior to them. He came across as arrogant, egotistical and full of conceit. I ignored his behavior and drove with him to my uncle's place. He didn't bother to come inside when we arrived. He was disrespectful and while that was a red flag, I pushed it aside. It showed how much I wanted things to work, even if I felt I was being disrespected or lied to. Respect was a notion I learned to embrace at a much later stage in my life.

Anil picked me up and we went on our first date to a pub that resembled a hole in the wall. A foul smell of urine pervaded throughout the establishment. No surprise, as they were no other diners other than us. In Hong Kong, a date isn't a pub meal let alone a restaurant of this standard, especially if it is the first date! The pub reminded me of a public urinal – not the most romantic place I had ever dreamed of.

After that, he drove us to a hotel and I didn't really understand what was going on. Naïve really. We got there and he said he wanted "some action". He got extremely forceful almost immediately. I pushed him away. Luckily, he calmed down and stopped. After this episode, I insisted that I be taken back to my uncle's place.

I felt violated yet again. I was still clinging to my warped notions of love. I didn't end things then and there, but I decided to keep my distance. Eventually, for some unknown reason, I gave the relationship another chance and agreed to go on another date with him. This time he picked me up from my cousin's place. They were flabbergasted when Anil just honked angrily from the driveway and didn't bother to come in. It made my cousin furious because he didn't show any respect towards my family.

In our culture, any average guy would know that to win a girl, he has to show appreciation of her family. He didn't bother to show any respect at all and that should have been the final straw. Despite this, I still ended up going to his house for dinner to meet his parents. They asked me a lot of questions and I felt like all of a sudden, I needed to work for their approval – like the ball was in their court. This was very confusing because Anil hadn't behaved well at all. I was starting to feel like I was being played. I went through the motions and behaved like a 'good Indian girl'. I was obedient and respectful to his parents at all times, even whilst I was being interrogated. I was polite and timid; traits which are supposedly good coming from a girl with a cultured upbringing. An Indian girl shouldn't be too outspoken or opinionated because then her new family will suspect she may speak her mind and cause trouble. When an Indian girl marries a guy, she is expected to adjust to his lifestyle and be malleable.

When I got back to Hong Kong, I told Anil I couldn't continue this relationship because he insulted my family. I made it clear that we didn't get along like I thought we would. He made no effort to be friendly to Mama or any of my cousins. His behavior told me how little he valued me. If he can act like my family are of no importance to him, then what can I expect of him after we are married? I felt cheated. Before we met, he said how much he wanted to meet my family and cousins, but he behaved in an entirely different way.

My ability to read men and know when I was being played was completely off. I was clearly sending the wrong signals and saying the wrong things. When I got home, I cried so much because I was so mad at myself. I didn't know where to learn the unspoken rules of dating. One thing I did know with each experience was that it only continued to get worse. If I kept up these kinds of relationships, it was only going to go downhill. I would end up completely shattered and have no choice but to stop and notice what I was doing wrong.

*   *   *

The journey of finding love was, in essence, a journey of self-discovery. I needed to work out what love is in order to know who I wanted to share my life with. I seemed to be attracted to guys who were charismatic and were very good at talking a good game. As I got more into fitness I found athletic men more appealing. I remember once I was on a date with a French trainer named Gabriel. Gabriel was a six foot black guy with an athletic build and a big broad smile. He had charisma that would light up the room. His smile made me weak at the knees. One night, I met up with him for drinks. I was so nervous beforehand that I couldn't really eat.

When I went to meet him outside the bar, I assumed it would be just the two of us. I was looking forward to seeing another side to him other than his role as a trainer. Unfortunately, when we got to the bar, there was a room full of people who turned out to be his friends.

At that time, I was extremely shy and awkward. There was an obvious language barrier as most of the people in the bar spoke French. I felt out of place and wanted the night to end! After what seemed like ages, but was in reality only two hours later, I went up to him and said, "I'm leaving." He didn't even once insist I stay and nor did he walk me out to the door. I felt humiliated and that left me feeling emptier than I had felt in a while.

I was so naïve because I assumed that if a guy asks you out, it will be just the two of you. But clearly that doesn't have to be the case. My meeting with him wasn't the date I had in mind. I had been anxious all day and excited because I thought I was going to get to know him better. When we were at the club, I was left alone most of the time, feeling shy and awkward in a room full of people. I wasn't introduced to anyone and nobody seemed interested in me. Hearing conversations and laughter all around me, I kept wondering what was going on. He gave no reassurance that he was into me.

In hindsight, I could have said something playful or just gone with the flow. But instead I got annoyed and allowed it to bother me. I instantly ascertained that he just wasn't into me the way I wanted him to be. When I got home that night, I wondered if he was trying to test me or figure me out by seeing how I would react in a crowd. I continued to see him at the gym and initially it was awkward. After a while, I learned to move on as the appeal for him faded in my mind.

I believed in love even if it meant I got my heart bruised a few times. After some time, I met another Indian, Ranveer, also from a Sindhi background. Ranveer had a military look with a crooked nose and disheveled teeth. He lived in Japan so there was less of a time difference. I met him when I was 31 and in my third year of university. Being in my 30s, I felt less pressure to settle down because I was already considered 'old'. In my culture, your 20s is the prime age to find someone and tie the knot. When you pass that age, it is perceived by many that you've lost your chance. At the time that I met Ranveer, I was also set to become a teacher. I had another year to complete my studies before I would graduate. After a few weeks of chatting with Ranveer, it was clear that we had a connection and he was keen to come to Hong Kong and meet me. I thought he must be serious about me to want to come all that way. Again, he ticked all the boxes so I felt this would finally be right. I was excited to meet him and show him my city.

We spent time together and got on really well. I felt like this could actually work. Everything seemed to be going in the right direction – there was chemistry, humor, and conversations. We enjoyed each other's company. After he returned to Japan, we spoke and everything was going well. But over one phone call, he said something that was a deal breaker. Those that know me understand that getting my degree was one of the most important things I had set as a goal for myself that year. Ranveer disrespected my ambition and told me that I should quit university, as he wanted us to get married later in the year. He thought it was pointless for me to continue my education because I'd be at home taking care of his parents and our future children.

I was gobsmacked and couldn't believe my ears. He didn't ask me what I wanted to do after marriage. He went ahead and planned what I was going to do without considering me. I thought to myself, "Why on earth would I spend four years of undergraduate studies to marry some guy and stay at home and cook lentils and roll out chapattis? We're not in the 70s!" I am a modern girl who wanted nothing more than to live out my dreams. He made it clear that he made more than enough money for both of us. There was no need for me to work.

After what was a heartbreaking chat, I ended the relationship. In the past, I had let men walk all over me. But, this time, I wasn't going to allow some guy to belittle me by telling me to give up on my dreams. As a child, I felt I had no control. As an old wound was being triggered, I was finally able to see it and take a stand – I was not going to allow another person to control my life. I had learnt my lesson and that was when I decided that I was done with Ranveer. The relationship was definitely over.

I've attracted all sorts of men into my life because I didn't ask the right questions early on or notice my insecurities.

Sometimes, it isn't about the questions you ask, but what the other person says or does. For instance, when Ranveer said, "You don't need to work because you'll be staying at home taking care of my parents, that is the role of an Indian wife," he reflected his opinion of Indian women. And so it became clear: Ranveer was not the one for me. Believe it or not, I am grateful! Ranveer was actually one of the men who taught me how to read the signs; to understand how a man was either violating or honoring me. My history with my father led me to overcompensate by giving far more than receiving in most of my relationships. I was too forgiving, and too willing to overlook the red flags. At the heart of it, I was insecure and believed that I didn't deserve to be loved.

This doesn't mean we should consistently measure how much we are giving. Instead we need to pay attention to whether we are doing all the 'work'. Is my partner also putting effort into the relationship, by being compassionate, comforting, kind, and most of all respectful?

Let's take Jon as an example. He was a great guy but, because of my own fear of him leaving me, I took the initiative to call or email all the time. If he didn't write back, I'd panic and follow up after a very short time. I didn't give him the chance to miss me. I let my fear dominate my thought process.

Jon, like the other guys I dated, didn't have to impress me much. They didn't have to put the effort in to get to know me. This became my pattern. I didn't quite realize that in pestering Jon, and falling victim to my own insecurity, I was actually creating a one-sided relationship. To be in a healthy relationship, the other person needs to be invested in it as well. In order for the partnership to work, it takes a guy to give and a girl to receive and vice versa. I was conditioned to be overly giving to the point that I put men on a pedestal. I didn't know how to receive because I didn't value myself or I thought that I didn't deserve to be given any love. When I stopped excessively giving, I noticed that there was nothing going on; the relationship would stagnate, fade and fall apart.

I met guys through friends and I was lucky that dating wasn't a problem. But going beyond the first stages of dating never really panned out for me. I felt I was constantly on a rollercoaster ride, and it was a rollercoaster that I couldn't get off. I was going round and round in circles, continuously wanting the ride to go elsewhere. The highs felt great but the lows stabbed at the very fabric of my heart. I felt lost because I didn't understand how to get out of the race of constant dating. I didn't want to just date, I wanted a man for life; a man who understood me and my values and everything I stood for.

Eventually, after I had taken some time off from my full-time teaching job and travelled extensively, I stopped chasing men. Getting away, having time to myself and being in new environments, helped me to see that enough was enough. Meditation helped me to figure out what I was doing and connect with myself. It guided me to understand who I wanted to be. A lot of soul searching and self-discovery were needed to figure out how to be with men and how to trust in what I deserved.

One weekend, when my friend and I decided to attend a weekend workshop in Hong Kong on self-care, philosophy and spirituality, I met someone special. This time around, I took my time to decide if I wanted to get involved with him. Through having a better sense of self, I had clearer standards. I was brave enough to be honest with him, especially after all of my previous dating fiascos. Unlike the other guys, he was interested in really getting to know me and made a lot of effort. He would email every day; long beautiful emails, which were open, deep and honest. When I was travelling, we would Skype and share our hopes and dreams about our lives. I saw a side in him that was endearing because he didn't mask anything about himself. He was very comfortable revealing to me who he was. Our love grew from a connection established through honesty and transparency. Before I knew it, we were in a relationship and I did something that was unheard of – I partially moved in with him. I stayed some nights at his place. That didn't go down well with my family at all, but I also knew that if I wanted this to work, I had to spend more time with him. He lived on an island and I lived in the city, so with work and a crazy city lifestyle, staying over was a necessary step to get to know each other on a deeper level.

Fast forward to today, we are happily married and that is because I put my feelings first and learnt to honor myself before the relationship. I wasn't a people-pleaser any more, and stopped seeking affirmation from outside sources. He taught me that finding true love was not about proving anything to each other, but rather loving one another through trust and friendship. He will always remain mine in my heart. When Big Mama met him for the first time in Barcelona, she knew I fell for who he was inside like she did with Papa.

Being with my husband makes me realize how alike he is to Papa; I'd like to believe they are very similar because I had tremendous respect and admiration for Papa. He loved the sea, adored nature and enjoyed his walks along the waterfront, just like my husband. Both of these men would do small things every day that show they care. Papa had a smile that would warm my heart, in the same way my husband has a warm smile that radiates from his very being. I have unconsciously chosen a man like my grandfather and I've become, in some respects, like Big Mama. I hope to one day love my man like she did hers.

Suffering

"Character cannot be developed in ease and quiet. Only through experience of trial and suffering can the soul be strengthened, ambition inspired, and success achieved."

— **Helen Keller**

As a child, whenever I used to cry, I was told I was weak and needed to stop immediately. The first time I realized I was being shunned for crying was when I was about six years old. Mama, my brother, and I were at a night market, which was always overflowing with people and, more often than not, excessively crowded. I was swimming against a flood of people who were as big as King Kong! I stopped to look at a cute panda keychain at a stall and, when I turned to speak to my mom, she was gone! I panicked, feeling overwhelmed, scared and abandoned. I was lost and didn't know what to do.

I walked around aimlessly searching for Mama and my brother. After what felt like an eternity, which was in reality just a few minutes, I found them. Relieved, I held onto her like a lost child does. My mom's reaction was one that I couldn't understand. She saw me sobbing and I told her I was lost, yet she wasn't fazed at all. She was indifferent to my plight. My suffering bore no relevance to her and she failed to understand it. Worst of all, she ignored my tears. Instead of comfort, she gave me a stony wall of indifference. This subconsciously told me that crying doesn't matter, and tears are a sign of weakness. As I got older, I learned to bottle up my tears even when I felt the need to let out my emotions. What point was there in crying?

When I was younger, crying was always perceived as a sign of fragility. Those who aren't strong enough end up crying in situations when they shouldn't. This is an odd point of view as crying takes strength, especially for those who aren't used to being vulnerable. Crying is a way of saying, "I need help and I'm not okay, please help me now." When we get a response such as "stop that now, you are so weak", or "why on earth are you crying, weakling?," we grow up believing crying is wrong and something we should never do. Nobody likes being called, or perceived as, weak. In my experience, fragility has always been viewed as negative, with a stigma of being incapable of taking care of oneself. Can bottling up so much emotion be a good thing?

I'm not saying we should cry in each and every situation. There is always a time and a place to express our emotions and tears. Overexpression can cause just as many problems as underexpression. If I go to the fridge, find there is no rice milk in it and begin to sob then that is an issue. Unless of course I am dying of thirst and that is the only available drink! If we cry too much, people generally begin to take us much less seriously.

In many societies, it seems we have been conditioned to be raised in a certain way with regard to showing strength, regardless of gender. Crying in general appears to be worse for boys. Boys are expected to have a strong front, always hiding what they are feeling because tears are meant for girls. The expression, "You're such a girl!" is considered an insult to the average boy. Yet when a girl is expressing her emotions by crying, that too isn't accepted. Society tends to discriminate against anyone who shows signs of honoring how they feel, especially when it comes to being vulnerable. This was evident in my household as a child.

When I was in primary school, I was teased and bullied regularly. I remember in Primary 6 there was a boy named James who would make fun of me by calling me the name *Kamachi*, a Taiwanese sport-shoe brand. He knew it would bug me because he was saying Kamachi with the implication that it was similar to my name, Komal. Kamachi was considered 'cheap' in cost and reputation and most kids would prefer wearing Puma, Nike or Reebok. Being called this brand name made me feel inferior and rejected. He didn't just bully me on his own, he'd say it and get others to join in or laugh at me. I felt isolated and inferior while he celebrated in my pain and anguish. I began to hate being the center of attention. I bottled the pain and suffering up inside and dealt with it quietly on my own. I didn't think my parents would care enough to do something, and indeed they responded to reports about the bullying with indifference. Similar to so many other instances in which I was left feeling desolate, alone and disconnected. I suffered in silence.

Over time, I learned to be like everyone else by rejecting my tears. When I cried it was done behind closed doors because I learned that many people don't want to be around someone who is suffering. I looked like a happy child and I wanted to keep that impression because being a smiley child draws people to you. Many nights as a child, I'd cry myself to sleep because things would just get too overwhelming and I didn't know how to cope. Tears were my outlet to soothe my pain. When you can't talk about emotions at home, it leads you to suppress any vulnerable feelings that surface, or try to deal with them on your own. Sadly, ignoring our suffering is something we do very well because looking at it straight in the eye takes extreme courage, which I certainly didn't have back then. Facing any suffering means accepting what is going on, whether it is domestic violence, depression, or abuse. Isn't it much easier to pretend it doesn't exist and carry on living rather than dealing with it?

When I was a child, facing pain was hard because a lot of suppressed emotions suddenly surfaced and I felt like I was drowning. I feared that, if I opened the can of worms, it wouldn't stop and I might get stuck in it for a long time. As a girl, especially an Indian in a school setting of students who were mainly Chinese, I didn't have the courage to express myself because I already felt different and alienated. So, it was best to ignore what was going on. Ignoring meant burying the pain as facing it meant life would stop.

I would often ask, in my quieter moments, "Why me?" Today, when I experience negative events I say, "what is this experience teaching me?" It took a long time to look at pitfalls with a different lens. Suffering is when we do not allow ourselves to be okay with feeling low. There seems to be a need to either ignore the negative state we are in and focus on what we can do about the situation – completely ignoring the fact that it isn't about the situation as much as it is about how we feel about it that matters. When we are okay with not being okay, then we are accepting our emotions whatever they may be, and that is one way of being kind to ourselves. Giving ourselves the permission to feel sad, to feel broken, or to feel happy but simultaneously confused about a situation that is troubling us doesn't make us wrong, it just makes us human. Letting ourselves feel is a way of being present with the state we are in so that this too can pass. It takes a shift in how we look at emotions and suffering for change to occur. There finally came a point where I could no longer pretend life was good and that was terrifying.

We are petrified when someone we know is suffering, for instance when our best friend was just dumped by her boyfriend, we will say something along the lines of, "Get over him, he's not worth your tears." Or we'd say something like, "See it's good that you know now, and you didn't waste any more time with this loser." What we aren't saying, which could help, is simply "how are you feeling?" The experience has happened, and there is an emotional reaction to it, hence the friend is suffering. Allowing the friend to go through the emotions are what will help her get through this phase and come out feeling better versus intellectualizing it or ignoring it and then moving on.

A few months ago, one of my students asked if she could have a chat, which I was more than happy to do. Many of the girls I teach come to see me when they are facing personal dilemmas and want to air it out and get some advice. I feel honored to be in a position to do that. Besides, having my high school teacher, Ms. Dobbs, be there for me back then when I needed her most, I feel even more inclined to pay it forward.

Let's call this student Karen. She came to see me and said that she was having problems at home. She explained how the school social worker was well aware of the case. She said that her father physically abused her and that it had been going on for some years now. She deliberately went home late but he was always at home because he didn't work and there was no one at home to protect her. My heart reached out to her. She explained that her mother worked and got off work really late at night, hence she was always alone at home with him. I suggested that she speak to her mom about it and explain how severe the situation was. But also to get the school social worker to put pressure on the mother to ensure her daughter was safe.

A few days after the new school year started and Karen was waiting around in the vicinity of the staff room. I was happy to see her as usual. She said she had good news to share. I was delighted. She said, "First I need to tell you something. I didn't tell you the whole truth because I knew you would be very angry."

I nodded so she could continue.

"My father would hit me but also touch me."

I looked at her, eyes wide, in complete disbelief. Yes, she was right, I was fuming. I wanted to make sure I heard her right, so I asked, "Touch? Do you mean sexually? Did he rape you? Did his penis go inside of you?" I wanted to be absolutely sure she understood what rape meant.

"No, he didn't. Just touch," she confirmed.

I felt a sense of relief but inside I was also seething with anger. She saw my expression and could clearly see an inkling of how I felt. At this point I thought it was fair to ask her some questions. I initially asked her if she told her mother. I then asked her why didn't she tell the social worker or me before? She said her mother knew now. The school social worker filed a case, her father was arrested and now it has gone to court. She is currently safe and living in a dormitory with her mother. She had a huge smile on her face from ear to ear and I could see that she wasn't just happy but relieved. She was sharing how happy she was feeling so I then altered my mood to be happy for her, relieved that she was finally free and safe.

For years, Karen had kept this to herself. She didn't want to burden her overworked mom, but deep down she was always the child that needed protecting. When she finally did pluck up the courage to tell her mom about the physical abuse, nothing changed. Her mom felt more obligated to her husband than her daughter. Whilst all of this was happening, Karen attended school, got good grades, and was a positive bubbly child. One would have never thought she had gone through such tragedy at the hands of her father. She reminded me of my experience and the power a father has over his child. My father, just like hers, got so caught up in his own twisted sexual issues and his own frustrations, that he didn't see the damage he was causing to his very own daughter.

Whilst her resilience might be high, she must have gone through the continued mental torture of not knowing when she would next get attacked. The stress that the body goes through is immense and the toll on the psyche is high. The level of pain she had to undergo also meant she had to suppress those feelings and emotions in order to be able to cope with her everyday life.

One of my friends, let's call her Jessie, calls whenever she's down and usually it's a 'boy situation'. There will be tears and after the crying session, whether or not the advice was useful, she feels better and moves on from the situation. She gives herself permission to cry and reaches out. However, if one is to judge her based on her social media profile, she would not come across that way. Jessie seems to be an independent and adventurous girl who enjoys travelling and has an exciting life! The reason is simply because some of us deem posting about our bad day or going through a hard time as negative or too serious and believe that it indirectly pulls other people down.

Facebook is a platform on which there are happy pictures and videos of animals, holidays, food, etc. and rarely does one post things about suffering because the idea with social media is as a virtual reality on which to have fun and connect with people, which I must say is a great tool. However, when there is just one side of the coin being shown more, we don't see the reality of what is truly going on in the lives of people that we care about. I was one of them. I would post vegan meals, my workout success, the brilliant day I had at work, etc. It was very recently that I started sharing the other side of me on Facebook on my *A Girl's Faith* page because I wanted to create a space where people can talk about anything that allows us to question our morals, whether it be rape, mental health, gender equality, or any other personal issues. In my opinion, showcasing a worldview that everyone has a perfect life seems to create more emotional distress because we end up feeling like we are the only ones struggling or in pain.

Over a decade ago, one of my distant cousins committed suicide. The speculation was that she was unhappy and it boiled down to feeling pressured to look a certain way so she could meet an eligible Indian guy and be married. Sadly, that never happened and her mind gave up on her. She was drowning in her pain to such an extent that she wanted out of this realm and her way to cope with suffering was to end her life.

My cousin's death horrified me. I wished I was closer to her and could have been there for her in her time of distress. She suffered in silence and never told a soul about what she was actually feeling. I was also upset at how there is a standard, a very narrow yardstick of how a girl or a boy should behave and anyone who doesn't fit that is made to feel like a reject. I wondered if she felt isolated and disconnected from her true self.

While I was writing my memoir, there was an occasion when I was walking from Discovery Bay, on another island in Hong Kong, to the ferry pier. I had had a brilliant day and was feeling pleased with myself. As I was crossing the road, my left foot buckled over. I stood there at the corner of the road, literally frozen, unable to move an inch. I was in shock, in extreme pain, standing at the corner of the road. I dropped all my bags (because I had been carrying three heavy bags) to examine my foot. I couldn't understand how my foot swelled in a minute to the size of a tennis ball! I tried to compose myself so that I could somehow walk the rest of the way to the ferry pier, which was roughly another three minutes away. The state that I was in, it would have taken me an entire day to walk there.

I saw two ladies, who appeared like they had just returned from a hike. I was smiling as usual and we greeted one another. I was reluctant to ask for help but I had to. My body was bent forward to assist my injured foot. One of the two ladies saw me struggling and came up to me. I told them what had occurred. Without a thought, they took my bags and lifted me from under my armpits. After a few seconds, we saw a lady in a golf cart. In Discovery Bay, regular cars are not allowed on the roads so many people drive a golf cart. One of the ladies crossed the road and approached the woman in the golf cart, asking her if she could give me a lift to the ferry pier. Luckily, she said yes and I was driven to the pier and got the help I needed until my husband arrived shortly after.

I was suffering, and while I am often terrible at asking for help, I had to put my shame aside and ask for assistance because I was in a dire situation. I was extremely grateful and, along the way, I got more help than I expected.

Aside from needing help, the experience of injuring myself, being immobile in a cast and being bed-bound taught me a lot about humility and suffering. When I was in the hospital, waiting to be seen, the pain was excruciating and I was upset at how it happened. But once I met the doctor and he explained that I had broken two bones in my foot, would have to stay at the hospital for a CT scan, and may require surgery, I realized I had to accept that I wasn't happy about it. I allowed myself to cry and feel weak. Once I was in the ward and the tears had settled, I was calmer. Being in the hospital gave me the chance to reflect on what this injury was teaching me and I have come to a few conclusions.

On a practical level, I was overdoing it by carrying more bags than I should (a bad habit of doing too much). I should have worn better shoes that would support my feet when I am physically juggling things. I now know that I also need to delegate more. On a spiritual level, it taught me to appreciate what I had taken for granted – what my body is able to do perfectly and yet it gets zero appreciation. It taught me to slow down and it is okay to not be a multi-tasker all the time. More importantly, it taught me to value the time I have because I can now slow down, appreciate the body I have because it will heal. And I gained more time than ever before to do things that bring meaning to my life. I have always lived life to the fullest and maybe my body was telling me to slow down and I wasn't listening – it was asking for help! Because it didn't get the help it needed, it had to break down so it was crystal clear to me that I had to pause and stop running on empty fuel.

My difficulty in asking for help stems from times when I was ignored, such as in the abuse I was being subjected to, or when I was disapproved of, like when my family made it clear they weren't happy with me applying to university. I never felt close enough to my parents to actually discuss my suffering during my childhood, or even now, as a rape survivor. Learning to rely on others when I was weak was allowing them to turn me away. Giving the power to someone else to say 'no' was hard, especially when I had experienced a fair amount of disapproval. But today, I'm learning to see that rejection is okay because I am finally trying to turn to people and that is a step in the right direction for my continued personal growth. Forgiveness is a deep-rooted emotion and can only begin to be given to others when you give it to yourself. Once I began to forgive myself for my past, I was able to reverberate this emotion around me. Through suffering, I realized that nothing of my past could be changed, but I could shift the direction of my future.

When Big Mama passed away, I was broken beyond belief. Initially I didn't invite anyone in to see my pain because I was steadfast in showing the world only my 'happy face'. A part of me didn't like to burden others with my misery, and another part of me was scared of being rejected if I reached out. Nevertheless, I still gave it a try and rang my friend. She was kind enough to meet me. We went out for a meal because she wanted to be there for me, and this felt good. What I learnt that night was an eye-opener. I've always been the shoulder for her to lean on, so when the tables were turned, it was hard because some people use their own story as a means to comfort others' pain. She talked about someone she knew who had passed away and the experience she went through. Sadly, her version of 'helping' me through my grieving process was unhelpful.

How I felt about my grandma's passing was different from, for instance, how my neighbor felt about his grandma's death. Our reactions towards a given situation are never quite the same, so what I needed was to be given the space to be vulnerable. But, instead, we talked about what happened as if my pain was being compared to someone else's. Suffering is subjective and personal and no exact experience is ever the same and, therefore, it cannot be compared. I felt like she had put my suffering into a box with hers, which took away the true essence of what I was feeling as a person. The dinner date left me understanding how little we know about talking about our painful emotions. We discussed the experience, but not about how I truly felt about the emotional pain of loss. The latter is what I realized helped me fundamentally to heal.

I didn't see a lot of dear ones pass away until I was in my late 30s. One early morning in December, my brother came into my bedroom, looking pale. My brother is not an early riser yet he stumbled into my room at four o'clock in the morning. He was holding the phone and I was confused. Without saying much, he handed the phone to me. "Hello?" I said, sounding groggy. Immediately I recognized the voice. My mind shifted gears and went into work mode; rummaging through my databank of information as to why I would get such an early morning call. It wasn't my birthday or Christmas yet so what was going on? Before I could ask, my cousin said, "Papa was in ICU and he passed away." I experienced the classic denial stage first and said to him, "That's not possible because we (my brother and I) just spoke to him a week ago." My cousin explained how it happened very suddenly.

My Papa was eating one moment and then he had a stroke and was taken by an ambulance to the hospital with Big Mama, and one of his grandsons (my cousin brother). That night, my grandpa was gone. As my cousin was relaying this to me, my mind was still trying to figure out how he could have died. He was perfectly fine when we spoke to him. I wasn't ready to digest all the information that was being fed to me from the other end of the phone line.

I'm known to be great at handling stressful, emotional situations and I can multitask like a wizard but, when it comes to a major crisis like death, my mind freezes because my brain cannot comprehend and process the information. It takes my brain a longer time to come to terms with what has occurred, so it either denies it or I become immobilized, not knowing how to react. After a minute or two, I was crying hysterically. There were so many life events Papa had yet to witness, and now that we were finally in a better financial situation, we wanted him to experience more of them. I felt like life was pulled out from under my feet. Papa was a father figure to all of his grandchildren and he was very close to all of us; losing him was an unprecedented time in my life and my first true experience of losing someone close to my heart.

I got dressed for work and went straight to the Principal's office. I explained how my Papa was like a father to me and that I needed to take a leave of absence to attend his funeral. I wasn't granted paid leave because it wasn't the death of one of my parents. I was going to be gone for two weeks so I understood that I had to take a pay cut during my absence. At that moment, none of that mattered. I just wanted to be there and be with Big Mama. I was also scared for her. "She must be devastated," I thought. Her life companion was suddenly gone. Big Mama and Papa did everything together. Big Mama never travelled without him. They were inseparable and I was terrified about how she was coping with not having him around anymore.

We arrived in Malaga, Spain, and I walked into the house, which was once a jovial home with of lots of joy, laughter and happy times together, but was now a home with a looming sense of grief that engulfed all of us. I was surrounded by relatives to mourn the patriarch of our family.

The house lost its sparkle and warmth and all I felt was pain and anger. Seeing Big Mama in white was hard to swallow. In Hindu custom, white is worn when someone in the family passes away. She wore white from thereon and seeing her suddenly alter her appearance from a woman who loved color, style, and being glammed up, to wearing no make-up and dressing in a white salwar kameez shook me. The reality of the situation hit home like a ton of bricks. I found myself in tears, not only because Papa was gone, but because Big Mama wasn't the same as I remembered her – vibrant, full of life and someone who knew how to hold the family together. I was in my 30s, and I was reacting like a child, shocked at how my pillar looked different. She no longer looked strong and in control and I was so afraid of what all that meant, and what the future would hold for her. Was she going to change now that Papa was gone? I didn't know how to be strong for her because she was *my* strength.

During this time, prayers and rituals were performed and being with family and turning to God for comfort and strength was essential. We were a united front, being there for Big Mama. With each passing day, she seemed stronger. Her years of faith in the Lord gave her the strength to accept the loss despite the pain she was facing. She allowed herself to weep like a baby and she gave herself permission to be weak when she had to. She was true to herself. I learned so much from seeing how she coped with Papa's death.

Big Mama's life changed when she moved to Barcelona to live with my uncle, her younger son, and his family. Her entire life transformed overnight and, while it was hard to adjust to all the changes, I admire her for going through with it. Many people give up when the loss of a loved one becomes unbearable. It amazed me how she was able to bounce back and her remarkable way of dealing with the circumstance undeniably gave me, as well as the whole family, hope. Her steadfast faith in understanding that life is unpredictable and that death is inevitable showed me that she was a woman of absolute strength. And through her suffering, she turned her pain around to foster a sense of understanding for what was ultimately meant to happen in her life. She also taught me that nothing lasts forever.

A decade later, in December 2017, I got a text that Big Mama wasn't well, and 'wasn't going to make it' I was in Bangkok at the time and took the first flight out to see her. She got better and I was lucky to have seen her because five months later, in May, she passed away. Unlike Papa's death, which was all very sudden to the family, with Big Mama's passing, we were somewhat prepared. At least, that's what I thought. I knew she was weak, I saw her fragile state even though she got better, I was mentally aware that she was 90 years old and she had lived a long and full life. What I understood mentally, I didn't comprehend emotionally because when I read the text that she had gone, it broke me again. It was then that I realized that we are expected to be prepared for death and that when we know someone is going to go, we should somehow find it easier to let go. Sadly, I learnt that this is not entirely true.

It wasn't because I couldn't accept the fact that she was weak and that her body couldn't continue living. It was realizing that I no longer would have someone like a mom, who loved me unconditionally, who was my pillar, who was in my corner, by my side, and always encouraging me to surge forward. Suddenly, I wouldn't have my matriarch.

Accepting her death was not the problem, it was the void that was etched in my heart. Knowing that her presence gave me hope and courage was the most difficult lesson in suffering I have endured in my life. Her passing made me feel like an orphan.

Rarely do I cry in front of my students but the morning I got the text, I was getting ready for work and I diligently went into school as usual. I acted the part, but felt like a zombie. I vividly remember how I conducted my class, behind a huge façade. Some of the students know me and allowed me to be vulnerable. I was handing them exercises, to prepare them for their upcoming exam and I was dazed, staring at the window, tears rolling down my cheeks. I then realized the students were all looking at me in shock. I wiped off my tears, with the back of my hand, and explained about the passing of my grandma. They had heard about her so they knew how much she meant to me. One girl walked to the front of the classroom, stood in front of me, gave me a tissue to wipe the remainder of my tears and hugged me.

For a while, I was so consumed with work that I didn't allow myself to get weak because the tears overwhelmed me and at times I found myself losing control. My husband reminded me of the need to cry because he knew that her influence on me had saved me from my inner pain of being raped. I would sit and stare at her picture and rewatch videos taken of her back in December. Tears rolled down my cheeks and I was sobbing until I couldn't cry anymore. I had days of going through this until I felt I could look at her and feel love and not sadness. Grieving isn't linear so there are days I would still cry for Papa too and I am okay with that because I have embraced suffering and not labeled it as something intolerable.

It is through suffering that I have learnt how much I am discovering about my life path. I understand that in life there has to be pain because that is the other side to happiness.

Through suffering, I learn how to be okay with how I feel even if it causes me discomfort.

Big Mama lived accepting the loss of her husband. Prior to that, she allowed herself to go through the stages of grieving. She didn't let her ego, or strong frontier, get in the way and by being true to what she understood life was, she was able to live in harmony with the dichotomy that life offers with both happiness and suffering. Almost like the Yin to the Yang – through balance, faith, understanding and acceptance.

Embrace Failure

"Failure is so important. We speak about success all the time. It is the ability to resist failure or use failure that often leads to greater success. I've met people who don't want to try for fear of failing."
— **J.K. Rowling**

When I was a little girl, Big Mama spent a great deal of time teaching me how to make chapatti. I failed on numerous occasions and have never been able to create chapatti that looked anything like hers. I laid the wooden rolling pin out with great care and attention. I added lots of *atta* (whole-wheat flour) so it didn't stick to the dough. I applied the right amount of pressure to it and rotated it just like she instructed. But for some unknown reason, her chapatti was always circular just like a tortilla but mine always ended up resembling the map of India! Long, oversized, with jagged edges and definitely not uniform.

In theory, a chapatti is supposed to be soft just like a tortilla. When I made my chapattis, they turned out chewy and a bit hard. They were like eating cardboard! I was devastated because I couldn't understand what I was doing wrong. Big Mama was patient with me, but she also expected perfection. My failed attempts did not go unnoticed. I didn't get the comforting reassurance I wanted because Big Mama was all about tough love. I wanted to hear, "it's okay *Beta* (my child), you'll get it next time. Keep trying." I saw her perform everything effortlessly, or so it seemed, so I wanted my work to reflect hers. I wanted my effort to match my outcome.

Even though my chapattis were a complete flop, Big Mama never believed in throwing away food. My oddly shaped, overly cooked chapattis were there in the chapatti box amongst the perfect ones at the dinner table. One time, Big Mama took out the one I made, and examined it carefully. I felt a sense of shame and embarrassment. She tore it in half and placed it on my plate and said she wanted me to try it. She said, "That is the only way you will learn." Big Mama believed that taste was vital in order to understand how to make a good chapatti. It was definitely a reflective exercise. She took one of the chapatti from the box and gave it to Papa to eat. He grimaced and agreed that mine needed more work. What shocked me was that she herself ate it and told me it didn't taste that bad. It was her way of both complimenting and encouraging me. I broke off bits of the chapatti and whirled it around the *daal* (lentil stew) on my plate. I gave it a try and it tasted like rubber because it had hardened. Big Mama, on the other hand, saw my effort and chose to support me on this culinary mission. She ate it like it was a perfectly rounded chapatti. She demonstrated love by accepting my flawed culinary skills, which in turn acted as a motivator for me to keep trying.

I failed and I didn't just fail once. It took months and many burnt and raw chapattis to get it right. There was a reason for me to keep going – to not give up – and that was because of Big Mama. Especially since she invested so much time and energy in helping me, the main reason I kept trying again and again was because she believed in me, which helped me to ultimately believe in myself. Eventually, after many months of failed attempts, I did it. I finally made an acceptable chapatti, which brought a huge smile to my face. I finally got a glimpse of what success tasted like.

* * *

The moment when success takes place, it is like magic. More often than not, we forget to relish that experience. When the hard work has finally paid off, we should soak up that success and enjoy the reward. That is the beauty of success. But far too often, we neglect to really flow with that feeling. When we let it in, we allow ourselves to be in the moment. We drink in the success and revel in it. The memory of this feeling helps to motivate us toward our next target.

The excitement is often short-lived. As we rush towards our next goal, we fail to remember the successes we achieved. Taking the time out to celebrate success also allows the mind to relax and have the time out it needs. Cultivating time for the mind to stop allows it to sharpen our ideas and efficiency. A rejuvenated mind can assist us with our plans going forward.

Some people tend to overexaggerate their success and plaster it all over social media. This creates an unrealistic view of how success is obtained. Social media promotes the victories of accomplished individuals. But rarely do people share how they got there. What struggles did they have to go through to reach that destination? This is something we rarely hear about. The images of success that are posted all over social media give us a false impression that success is achieved overnight.

We don't get the chance to see failure as part of the process. It often takes hard work, patience and commitment to truly succeed. To think people are always successful at the first attempt is unrealistic. The tough journey of achieving the dream that we desire takes a number of tries before it comes through.

When I was in my early 20s, I was unaware of my future career path. My dream was to go to university and study journalism or writing, but that didn't happen so I ended up jumping from job to job. Not having a skillset to offer a workplace affected my self-esteem. I didn't see how I could do a job correctly and contribute to anything meaningful. Nevertheless, I got lucky and someone from the religious organization I was involved in was looking for a secretary. I thought this chance might change the course of my life! I was such an idealist!

I got offered a job at a reputable barrister's chamber. The firm was looking for a secretary to work with three different barristers. I was so elated about being offered this job. In particular, I really admired one of the barristers. His name was Deepak. He was a well-groomed, sophisticated Indian man with flair and panache. It couldn't have been a better opportunity. God was answering my prayers!

A few weeks later, I got the job after the standard protocol of interviews. I felt extremely sophisticated working in an office surrounded by oak furniture and a grand reception area. It had a classy colonial British feel to it with a sophisticated sofa setting at the reception. Not to mention, it was located in one of the finest buildings in Hong Kong. Walking to work made me feel like I had finally made it in the workforce.

I was assigned to a spacious cubicle right behind the receptionist. My work involved answering phone calls, scheduling appointments and doing basic computer-related tasks. When I had nothing to do, I was told I could do whatever I wanted! How rare was that?

Hearing what my job entailed, one would think I'd have no problems. It was an ideal job for someone as green as I was. Unfortunately, before my probation was up, I was told that I wasn't going to be offered a permanent position. I was pretty upset by this. So what had I done? On one occasion, one of the barristers asked me to photocopy sections of a legal reference book onto A4-sized paper. I didn't know how to work the photocopier, so I didn't feel confident about the situation. I figured A3 sized paper would be better in theory because it was bigger so it would be easier to read. I returned to my desk, feeling a sense of relief having completed this complicated task. The barrister was livid and shocked at my perceived uselessness. I managed to screw up a basic task that even a teenager could do with ease. He was in a massive hurry to go to court and here I was fussing around a photocopier. I wanted to dig a hole and bury myself in it because I felt like a huge failure. He strolled up to the photocopier, with me by his side. He was clearly furious and was muttering under his breath. I stood there sheepishly feeling like a school kid who was being told off.

Unfortunately, I continued to make mistake after mistake after mistake. One day, the phone rang and the person on the other end was looking for a barrister that I was working for. I had to take a message because he was on another call. I politely asked for his name and contact details. That shouldn't have been difficult but shockingly, it was. I managed to mess that up too. The caller said his name but because it was a complex name, one that I hadn't heard before. I didn't know how to spell it. I was too embarrassed to ask given he was a regular caller. I started panicking and I couldn't catch his name. I was busy trying to spell it but my hands were quivering and I couldn't catch my breath. Before I could calm myself down, my intercom button rang. "Who was that?" The barrister inquired. He was aware that his other line had rung. I fumbled through words, scared of what to say because this was a total disaster. I read to him what I had scribbled down. He was confused about what I was muttering. He hung up and walked out of his office. I was now terrified, afraid to face him and fearing the consequences.

I was angry at myself because I felt I shouldn't have made any more mistakes. In my eyes my blunder meant I was completely inadequate. I found myself taking it personally. I shrunk and sat there with my head resting slightly on my desk. He looked at my telephone message pad and was horrified at my incompetence. Without saying a word, he went up to the receptionist. He asked her who had called, since many calls get transferred through reception. Luckily, she recognized the caller's voice and knew exactly who he was. I was relieved, but still in a dilemma. I was hoping the barrister would say something so I could put this behind me, but sadly he didn't. It was harder to move on because I was uncertain about what he was thinking or what he was going to do about it, if anything at all.

I failed terribly as a secretary at this law firm because I didn't feel I could perform basic tasks that were assigned to me. I took my failed attempts personally and didn't have the maturity to learn from them. With every task I did my performance only got worse. This led to me actually losing the very job that I initially cared so much about.

Failure is simply the stepping-stone to getting where we want to be. What stops us from progressing is how we respond to failure. As a legal secretary, I failed at my job because I took it personally and that ate me up inside. I didn't go to work with a mindset of curiosity and eagerness to learn. I went in feeling out of place and awkward. I allowed feelings of inadequacy to spread into everything I did. Feeling like a failure was a result of how I felt about myself, which in turn affected everything I did. My mindset was the cause of the numerous bad experiences I encountered at work.

* * *

Over the years, I have worked hard on getting rid of negative self-belief. This eventually allowed me to experience success, and also learn from the errors that inevitably occur.

I adopted a positive mindset by being grateful for what I had. Learning to see experiences from an objective standpoint rather than a subjective one allowed me to step back and appreciate what was truly going on. By letting emotions take over, I became immune to reason, which cascaded into a series of self-deprecating opinions about myself. When I stepped back and looked at what the experience was trying to teach me, I was able to learn from it and grow more effectively.

The famous boxing film *Rocky* contains a particular quote, which I keep coming back to: "It ain't about how hard you hit. It's about how hard you can get hit and keep moving forward. How much you can take and keep moving forward. That's how winning is done!" These lines from the movie speak to me on many levels. First, because I love boxing so the inspiration of being in the ring and staying strong when you're getting hit is vital. And the same applies to life. Being knocked down in life is a natural phenomenon. Failed attempts happen and it is about how I react and bounce back that determine everything. I've learnt a great deal from those failed experiences. These experiences have been invaluable lessons that helped me surge forward. During my time at the barrister chambers, I may have failed but I learnt a valuable lesson. I have to want to fight (learn), to be the best version of myself (in the work that I do), so I could serve and be proud.

About six years ago, I attended my little cousin's wedding in Portugal. It was a beautiful destination wedding in the Algarve. There were golden beaches and breathtaking cliffs. I loved being in a new country, being exposed to its culture and combining it with a wedding was the cherry on top. Like many girls, I enjoyed being glammed up and around relatives and family. Indian weddings stretch four to five days, which involves prayers, an engagement ceremony, henna party, dance party, and the wedding reception. An Indian wedding is one big fat party in which everyone dresses up in their most glamorous formal Indian outfits, glistening from head to toe.

As the family of the groom, we arrived at the hotel where the wedding was going to take place days before the occasions commenced, and before the guests arrived. Since all of the cousins live in different countries, reuniting was a celebration in itself. We partied all night like we never had. It was our first time in the Algarve and we wanted to paint the town red with the groom and so we did. We were all heavily intoxicated, having mixed all sorts of alcohol and shots. I was buzzing and usually when I've had quite a bit to drink, I'm like a kangaroo, jumping around. We bar-hopped and at one of the clubs, I met a guy, Khaled. He was 5 feet 10 inches tall, with a sun-kissed tan and wavy dark brown hair. Khaled had big deep brown eyes in which one could get lost. I recognized him, but couldn't place him. Feeling confident, thanks to the vodka and tequila shots, I pulled him to me on the congested dance floor. We were inches away from each other. Our eyes met and we got lost in gazing at each other. I felt something; a spark perhaps, but then I thought it might have been the drinks because soon after, he walked out. Although gutted, I continued to dance the night away.

The next day, with a massive hangover, all the family members gathered to prepare for the first ceremony. Khaled was history and that was that. Before I knew it, I saw him again, at the hotel we were staying at, behind the counter. That was when I realized that that was where I had first seen him. The night we checked in, he was behind the reception area, checking us in. I saw him, but pretended to be cool because I assumed he wasn't interested as he walked away the night before at the club. He smiled at me and I smiled back. I felt something, but ignored it again because, I thought, he clearly didn't like me. I proceeded to meet my family and got busy with the wedding preparations.

The wedding came and went. We had a gala time. The guy was around and we smiled back and forth but that was it. I was disappointed, but I didn't think it was realistic because I was at my cousin's wedding and here was this random guy who worked at the hotel that I had a moment with at the club. Such encounters are common in clubs, I justified to myself. Whatever this feeling was that we seemed to have, couldn't go anywhere because I live in Hong Kong!

As soon as I left Portugal, I got a message from him on Facebook. I was surprised that he even knew my name! He had my cousin (the groom) on his friend's list and he found me. Our friendship started and we exchanged messages and calls frequently. I thought he walked out of the club that night because he wasn't interested in me. It turned out that he was unsure if I was single. He assumed I was seeing someone because of the crowd of guys around me – who were part of the wedding party – and that I pulled him to the dance floor because I was giddy from the festivities.

Our chemistry was real, but also short-lived. We had a great time chatting and had quite a lot in common. But most importantly, we felt relaxed and comfortable with each other. But after a few weeks, I didn't believe it could happen because it felt too good to be true. Here was an Algerian-Portuguese guy out of the blue, interested in an Indian girl who was a decade older, living on the other side of the planet. I started doubting that a solid connection could ever happen and my doubt turned into giving up on the very thing I wanted – love.

I wanted us to have something, but I wasn't willing to go with the flow because I didn't think it would work out. I didn't trust the distance. I was convinced he would break my heart. So I proceeded with my classic routine: I walked away gradually, playing it cool as a protective mechanism. I told myself that it was a holiday fling, that he would have moved onto another, prettier girl. Besides, why would someone like him want to be with an older Indian girl? I didn't believe it was going to happen because, if it was supposed to be then it would have been. Thanks to *Pretty Woman,* I had this crazy unrealistic notion of romance and relationships. When Richard Gere drove down Julia Roberts' street and went up the ladder with a rose in his mouth, to be with her, it melted my heart. Despite all the challenges, Richard makes her his top priority and their romance blossoms. I was telling myself, it's not like Khaled is moving countries to be with me so clearly he wasn't as interested as I thought. My crazy philosophies made it justifiable to not commit fully to getting to know him. Getting my heart broken was too much to risk, so I decided not to try. I chose to let him go than to see where life could take us.

I never knew my experiences in dating were because I feared failing and that I lacked patience. I thought maybe I was picky, or perhaps I was scared of letting someone in and then discovering that he would say the standard line, "It's not working out". But deep down, failure had a lot to do with it. I was scared that I would give it my all and get my heart broken, which to me translates into failure. To avoid getting myself into that state, I was committed but only for a short period of time. I set an expiry date in my mind as soon as I started dating someone. And if it didn't progress in the way I wanted then I would walk away. The sad truth was that Khaled had no clue that I had all these steadfast and occasionally damaging unspoken rules.

I didn't have the patience and I was too scared to fail that I let what could have grown into something beautiful slip away. I didn't want to take chances. I wanted to be assured because I didn't like risks. Risk involved not knowing and losing some semblance of power. I wanted to be fully in control and I wanted to know where it was going and what was happening. What I felt for Khaled was real and because it was, it allowed me to reflect on what I wanted and it opened the path to something better. I was presented with another chance and met an amazing guy, my husband and this time I had learned what not to do and to go with the flow and see where it took us.

Patience is what is lacking in today's society, whether it be in a relationship, writing a book or becoming successful in a business, it all takes fortitude. When I first started writing this memoir, I knew it was going take many months – but honestly I had no clue how consuming it would get even though I had done it before. The last time I wrote a book, I wrote it over a period of years whereas this time, because I found an agent to work with and we agreed to a realistic timeframe, it has taken less than a year. There were times it was difficult and emotionally taxing. It was less difficult in regards to the writing and more relating to the feedback I got from my first line editor, Max. With each chapter I sent to Max, he would send it back with feedback. The first few chapters he sent back he repeatedly wrote, "sloppy writing. Follow a linear timeline and use elevated vocabulary." I had no clue what he meant so the best thing to do should have been to ask, but I was busy at work, so I let it be. We know that when we ignore something, it doesn't just go away. The next chapter was due and again I got something similar. To be honest, I didn't even bother to digest what Max was trying to show me, because I was impatient and didn't understand my commitment as an author.

I just wanted to write so I did what I knew, which was to type away, and didn't spend the time to understand what he was trying to teach me. As any editor would do, Max stuck to what he said and kept throwing those comments back to me until one day I cried. I sobbed hard because this time, the words stood out more when he replaced 'sloppy' with 'lazy' and as a teacher, I know when my student is being lazy with their work, it shows a lack of commitment. It made me feel like Max thought I didn't care enough. I had a flashback of being in high school when I had Mr. Dubois' class. If I was struggling with one of his assignments, I would do the bare minimum just to get it done. I'd also copy if I had to especially if I didn't understand what to do. I liked Mr. Dubois, so making some effort in his classes was important to me. Max's repeated comments felt like he wasn't pleased with my work. Like a schoolgirl, I had let my teacher down. That hit me like a ton of bricks because I felt like I was a lousy writer. But it wasn't because I was a terrible writer; rather, it was more because I felt like a failure. I was trying to write and I was getting some criticism for it. I was forgetting the fact that it was actually constructive. I let my ego get in the way. Max was doing his best to help me become a brilliant writer.

I was pretty upset so I turned to my mentor, Pashmina, in order to alleviate the issue. I made it clear where I was stuck and looked at his comments objectively after I had calmed down. But the moment I looked the 'problem' in the eye, I accepted that I needed to change; the door to success started to open. It was then that I went through each comment he wrote patiently, and decided to be present with what was in front of me versus being caught up in my own emotions and that was when the chapters began to flow better.

The problem is, very often when I want something, and for me it was to get my memoir published and for it to be a bestseller, but I had to understand the implications of the commitment to that goal. But, the question of "how much am I willing to sacrifice to achieve it?" kept bouncing around in my mind. What are we willing to do for success to come to fruition? I was cutting corners because that is what I had learnt in life. But I wasn't fooling anybody, definitely not myself or my editor, who knew when I was writing at my best and when I was being lazy and careless.

Failure is something we don't talk about because we are embarrassed by how much we have not achieved. We associate it with what we haven't accomplished as a sign that we aren't skilled in that area or smart enough. We take our failure personally and feel we will be judged so we refuse to share it. On the contrary, failure is the very path towards triumph and learning about success. It is with each failure that we get closer to where we want to be. I want to celebrate my failure because it has led to my conquests. I will continue to fail because it doesn't take just one attempt to get something right that is worth doing.

Looking at how much I've learnt, it is truly a humbling experience because each time something hits me and I wake up realizing that I have fallen for the trap of quick gratification, I check myself. Big Mama was a perfectionist and what that meant was she took her time in everything she did until it became second nature to her, just like her skillful chapatti making. To me, it looked like a gift she was born with. But in actuality, she had an attitude of resilience. She never gave up, especially on me, and that is why her teachings taught me about the skills of learning through constantly improving myself.

PART TWO

Felix The Cat Was A Trap

"Experience is not what happens to a man;
it is what a man does with what happens to him."
— Aldous Huxley

As a child, I loved Felix the Cat – a funny black-and-white cartoon character with huge white eyes and a black body. My childhood friend, Amy, had an abundance of Felix the Cat paraphernalia when we were in Grade Seven. Kids do and say the silliest things sometimes; one day, Amy started a 'Felix the Cat Club' and nominated herself as the chairperson. Only those who owned Felix the Cat items could belong to this exclusive club. Seeing her adorned with Felix the Cat stationery, clothes, bags and handkerchiefs, made me want to be a part of it, too!

I loved Felix so much that I would plead with my parents to buy me anything related to him. I ended up having more stuff than I could imagine and throughout my childhood I collected bright yellow pajamas, a steel pencil case, stationary, mug, hair accessories, plastic plates, and much more. Sadly, in Hong Kong, My Melody and Hello Kitty were more common and I could barely get my hands on Felix the Cat products. Luckily, my father visited Japan often and Felix the Cat was huge there, so when he travelled for business trips, he would return with goodies for me and I'd be elated. I would feel loved because he seemed to indicate to me that he was thinking of me.

Upon returning from one of his business trips to Japan, he gave me a Felix the Cat stuffed toy. The plush cat was probably two-feet tall, black and white and very soft – perfect for cuddling whenever I needed some love.

I was territorial with my possessions and I didn't like people using or touching my things without asking. My mom loved teasing me because she knew it would wind me up. She'd take my stuffed cat and either hold it or, at times, hide it and I would often become hysterical. Being surrounded by the things I cherished was soothing and I liked being left alone with them. I was in a happy bubble and content when I was with my stuffed Felix reading one of my novels.

One day, I was taking a nap in my bedroom and, when I got up, I saw my mother throwing my Felix the Cat stuffed toy to my brother as a tease. I started to cry. My cat was my source of love and affection. Her attempt at humor associated with taking my things would upset me and I never found her antics funny because I felt something that was mine, that I owned, should not be taken without my permission. It hit a wound that, at that time, I had no clue about.

I took care in storing the things I valued. I kept my treasured Barbie dolls in their boxes so they wouldn't get damaged or dusty. They were stockpiled on top of my white wardrobe. It was impossible for me to reach so I'd climb on top of a drawer to reach the top of the wardrobe.

Getting the dolls down each time felt like I was receiving new presents that hadn't been opened before. I'd carefully place all the Barbie dolls on my bed, slowly opening each of them with precision, and removing them from the boxes. Each Barbie was treated like a princess while I changed her outfits, brushed her hair and embellished her newly combed hair with accessories. I had a chance to be a child and get carried away into the fairytale life of *Cinderella* and *Prince Charming*. Being with them allowed me to escape from my own world and pretend to live in a place where I felt loved and belonged. In my doll world, there was no danger or any kind of pressure to conform.

One day, my father told me that it was pointless to collect any more 'silly Barbie dolls,' as I was not a baby girl anymore and that it was best to give them to my half-sister, Rani. I had taken extensive and precise care of my collection of dolls and I wasn't ready to give them up. Yet, without warning or consent, my pristine Barbies disappeared from my life and I felt that they had been abducted – kidnapped – for Rani's home. My heart shattered into a million pieces the day I saw all of my dolls being taken away. Once again, tears flooded my eyes as rage began to collide with pain. I thought over and over again: "If Dad says he loves me, why can't he see that these dolls actually mean something to me?" His inability to see what was important to me made me feel like I wasn't good enough. I felt replaceable, in one instance, by Rani.

A few years ago, when my husband learnt about this story from my past, he surprised me by getting me five gorgeous brand-new Barbies! One of them was an Indian Barbie in an Egyptian blue chiffon sari with gold embroidery and she was stunning. I put her on a pedestal, literally and figuratively. Admiration for this beautiful doll transported me back to my childhood. I felt connected to the little girl in me, who felt calm, happy and at peace.

When my father took my dolls away, I felt he was forcing me to grow up against my will, because he wanted me to. It made more sense to my father when my dolls were gone because, in his mind, I was no longer a little girl, which justified his warped decision to do what he did to me when he would frequent my bedroom. My innocence as a little girl was slowly being chipped away. My father used to tell me convincing stories about how I needed to grow up, and encouraged me to stop being 'a little girl', because, according to him, staying in this realm was unhealthy and he would remind me of that by saying, "Komal, you need to grow up, it's for your own good."

*   *   *

I hardly considered my brother during those times. My father would habitually buy me gifts, whether it was Felix the Cat toys, Barbies or nice clothes or fruits from Japan. The sweet and juicy fruits he brought back from abroad were so luscious, but very expensive. My mom would constantly tell him that he was spoiling me by buying me too many things. I saw this as her not wanting me to be happy. In reality, what he was exhibiting was blatant favoritism. I can't remember a time when my father bought any presents for my brother. I actually can't remember a time when my father did *anything* kind for my brother. I never questioned it then. I often wonder how it made my brother feel to see that *his* father was constantly showering love upon his sister, and receiving so little.

My brother, although not close to my father, did receive a tremendous amount of affection from my mother. In the dynamic of our household, it seemed somewhat fair. I thought favoritism was normal in families because, as a child, I would hear, "Who do you love more, Mommy or Daddy?" I got asked that a lot by relatives, so it seemed normal that a parent would choose to like one kid over the other. It was when I was older that I realized how warped this was. As a kid, I felt special and was partially oblivious to the fact that my brother felt left out or unloved. While my brother was probably feeling all this and more, I felt pampered and special. The sad truth is, I was so wrapped up in my own bubble of happiness, I didn't notice how he truly felt. In hindsight, I wish I had paid attention to how awful he must have felt to experience such differences in attention from both our parents.

As a child, I didn't dig deeper into the meaning behind these presents. Most of us think happiness comes from what we have – material things – so these were things that gave me temporary joy. However, all of my father's showering of gifts seemed like there was a silent deal that I hadn't agreed to. A deal that cost me more than these presents were worth; it cost me nearly my life. It took years of therapy to understand the damage he had done. For years, I'd cry myself to sleep, feeling hollow, with recurring nightmares of falling off a cliff. My dreams seemed to be telling me to jump off and die. Later on, I learnt that it meant I was afraid of what could be ahead of me.

A few years ago, I fell in love. I met a man and, for the first time, it felt effortless and uncharacteristically right. Admittedly, as all couples do we go through our ups and downs, but together we have worked through them and it has made us stronger. However, one of the challenges of getting close to the man I fell in love with had a lot to do with my father; a pact I had no idea I had made. In theory, physical intimacy should not have been an issue between my husband and I. However, there were some obvious issues and concerns we faced when we connected on a physical level.

During that time, I started seeing a counselor, Michelle. Her initial thoughts were that I needed to loosen up because of my upbringing. She asked me specifically about my upbringing and how this rule of remaining a virgin until marriage had affected my life. I revealed how my body reacted during the act of sex. I told her that I had no control over my vagina. It was like my vagina had a mind of its own. The moment a 'foreign object' came in, my vagina – which I referred to as 'she' – tightened. The weird thing was that I had no clue 'she' was doing that.

My mind was saying okay, but my sexual organs were not. My physical side had its gates closed. I hadn't understood how 'she' worked or how 'she' felt because for years I didn't know her. I didn't stop to notice how 'she' felt during the act of sexual intercourse. I didn't stop to think about what 'she' went through as a child to cause a lack of trust in letting anyone else come in, since it rarely crossed my mind that 'she' had been abused.

Michelle and I began talking about my past, including the men I had dated and the men I was sexually active with in order to redefine and get down to the bottom of this mystery associated with my sexual organs. I shared some ghastly stories about the men I had dated. That didn't seem like we had reached the cause. Michelle kept asking questions, kindly and sensitively. I trusted her, and eventually I went on to divulge that my father sexually abused me. Michelle asked details of what I remembered and, when we were discussing the details, we discovered that what I had thought, and what actually occurred, were quite different.

For years I hadn't thought I was sexually abused. He touched my breasts, my vagina, went down on me, and put his penis inside of me until he orgasmed. This went on for years. Why didn't I think it was rape? Because he had said, "Komal, it is important you learn what to do when you become a wife. It is your duty to make your husband happy when you are older." Additionally, it was drilled into me that Indian girls were to remain a virgin until they got married, so I naturally assumed I was still a virgin. Why would I think otherwise? I mean, he was my father! And he was apparently teaching me how to be a woman. So I never questioned his actions or his motives.

My father constantly told me that he was educating me and that he didn't come inside of me so, therefore, I was still a virgin. These were tricks he used so he could continue to manipulate me. It was through counseling with Michelle and her asking me all the right questions that my father's dark side as a pedophile began to emerge. She asked me, "What did he do when he was laying next to you? Where was his penis when he was in the bed with you?" Did he put his penis inside you?" I answered, "yes" to all of her questions. I had never looked at it for what it was because I had complete faith in what he said. It was then, for the first time, when I connected the dots and heard what I was saying out loud to Michelle. My own confessions resonated in my ears and it hit me that this didn't make sense, because what I went through wasn't just sexual abuse. It was incest, and rape.

During my sessions with Michelle, I was beginning to see the truth. Learning about what had happened to me, and acknowledging the truth, was a painful and slow process. I was numb initially as a feeling of shock overwhelmed me. I was trying to process how this could have happened without my knowledge. I had learned to accept that I was sexually abused but rape was a completely different concept in my mind. I couldn't comprehend how it was possible that I was raped, yet was made to believe that I wasn't.

Processing the sheer scale of manipulation that had taken place was the hardest part for me to truly digest. I had been so desperate for parental love that I had believed and accepted whatever I was told. One of the most difficult parts was realizing that he simply didn't see me as his daughter. How could he see me that way, when he was in a sexual relationship with me? I felt a great sense of betrayal as the enormity of the situation sunk in. My psyche inwardly groaned as I tried to digest the full scale of what had taken place.

These realizations spilled outward into my sense of self and my relationship. I felt completely violated, and that I was no longer 'marriage material.' I was now branded as broken, used and unwanted. My self-esteem plummeted to an all-time low. I felt used. Not being a virgin meant I wasn't pure. In my mind, pure meant to be pristine like my Barbie dolls. But I was the furthest thing from pure, because I had lost my virginity to my father. I was raped so it made me feel dirty, unworthy and ashamed of myself. I was told that, as an Indian girl, I was meant to preserve myself for my husband and, if I was touched by someone else, I was no longer good enough and would be branded a slut. When I learnt that I lost my virginity as a young girl, every cell in my body caused me to reject my very existence.

I remember one day, after therapy, I was experiencing so much anger. I was enraged and all I wanted to do was to cut off his penis. I wanted to remove the symbol of what made him a man. To me, it seemed an appropriate punishment for what he had done. Somehow, among all my anger, I was also ashamed of feeling angry because, as a good daughter, I should respect my parents and, in the back of my mind, I always wondered if I had somehow invited this into my life. Michelle explained that I was a child, and that my father's primary role was to protect me. I was allowed to feel enraged and it was more than permissible to have these thoughts. I finally had consent, from myself and from my therapist, to get as angry as I wanted, which helped me work towards feeling better and whole.

The rage was so intense that one day that I called my father. I was screaming, fuming, yelling at my father for what he had done to me. He was not expecting a sudden international, long-distance phone call but I needed him to comprehend the pain he had caused me, the manipulation and lies that I could now see clearly. I went on to tell my father that I could press charges against him because of what he had done.

He told me how he was proud of my success, that I had a great job, lived in a nice place and that I found a good man to marry. In his eyes, my life had panned out well. It felt like he was trying to take credit for my successes when he had delayed them. He spoke like he cared because he used his charm to try and win me over again, conveying with the tone in his voice how he was happy for me and that he only wished me well and prays for me. I knew he didn't care because if he did, he would have shown how apologetic he was through actions and his words; he would have admitted how wrong he had been to do what he did, he would have paid the thousands of dollars for the years of therapy, stepped up to be a different man and a better person to show me that he was truly sorry. But he did none of that.

After what felt like months of experiencing, expressing and releasing all the anger I rightfully felt, I had to come to terms with the fact that my first sexual experience was in fact rape. Most girls remember their first time and talk about how painful it was or how they thought they loved the guy and can laugh about it years later, but I didn't have that privilege. I used to find it awkward when my friends would talk about sex they had with their partners because I had yet to figure out how I could be intimate in my own relationships and not feel violated. The hurt was overwhelming.

Penetration without consent is rape. It was, and is, as simple as that. A child cannot possibly give consent. I had thoughts of wanting to take him to court. I wanted him to grieve and feel shame for his actions because I had suffered for so many years. I was so angry at him and I wanted *him* to experience pain. I now know that this is a normal, and common, part of the process of grieving sexual abuse.

I had the chance to reflect, and after working through my emotions, I realized what I truly wanted for myself. I craved healing and to live a happy life. I didn't want my life to be focused on him. Pressing charges would mean a huge stressful ordeal and that was the last thing I wanted to deal with. The repercussions of having to fight him in a legal system did not sit well with how I envisioned my journey ahead from a girl to a woman. I just wanted him out of my life for good.

*   *   *

Pedophiles are people who are sexually attracted to children, though they may or may not act on it. Pedophiles have a neurobiological defect in their brains, which affects their behavior. Not all pedophiles molest children because some have stronger impulse control (Langevin, Wortzman, & Wright, 1989). My father was not in that category. My father was a 'preferred child offender' (Lanning, 2001), which means he turned to me even though he had another woman he was sexually active with. He raped me while he had other sexual relationships and, because the abuse continued for years, it was something he preferred – he chose to do it.

Situational offenders (Lanning, 2001) are those who are anti-social and abusive and often can be labeled as alcoholic and violent. This is sadly very common in households where parents, siblings, or relatives sexually violate children. These family members are usually abusive individuals and lash out at the kids. 'Preferred child offenders' have poor impulse control when in extremely difficult situations. On top of that they can also be controlling of others. These offenders are great with kids and they have a natural ability to be good around children because children gravitate towards them. From an outsider's perspective, my father seemed an ordinary man who was kind to people and was quite pious. He made an effort to put on a good public persona. His behind-the-scenes antics would never be revealed until I plucked up the courage to expose him. To get what he wanted, he used charm, which is very common for sexual offenders. In fact, charm was his main weapon.

As a girl, I was lured in by the presents he gave me. I was manipulated by his words. He would say, "Komal it is your

153

duty as a wife to please your husband, and I will show you how." This was like a mantra he used and it must have worked because I remember it so clearly. I felt it was my job to satisfy a man and my own needs or wants were unimportant. This belief leaked into every aspect of my life. I felt my needs were less important and therefore I tended to look out for others and make sure everyone else was happy before me.

*   *   *

Some people look at me now and wonder how could I have transformed from being so angry and hurt to where I am today? Firstly, I have to say, it took years. Initially, I blamed myself, then Sharon, then my father, then my mother and then, after some time, I had to accept what happened, and that I couldn't change any of it. There was no explanation that could satisfy my mind so I had to accept that the trauma of rape took place. Acceptance came from talking about it to my family and refusing to hide anymore. It also helped that I told my father that I could see the ugly truth in what he had done, and let him know how it had destroyed my relationships with men and, more importantly, myself.

Once I allowed myself to stop hiding, I opened myself to the truth and to the path of healing. While it was terrifying at times, I was feeling stronger with each past hurt I was forced to revisit. I was afraid that no one could ever love or accept me if they knew the whole truth. When I came out and said it aloud, I felt like the weight of the world had finally lifted from my shoulders. The need to acknowledge the truth was not just for myself, but for the people around me. I needed emotional support and I didn't want to hide in my pain. Receiving support from people like Michelle, my counselor; my high school teacher, Shakti, with whom I reconnected a few years ago, and in speaking to her, picked up where we had left off when I was 17. Last but certainly not least, the very person who has given me wings so I can fly and be the woman I am today, is my dearest husband. His support has opened up a pathway of trust and has paved the way to recovery, allowing me to trust in the process of forgiveness. These people, who are my angels, have helped me soar to new heights with regard to my own self-development. Their need to protect me has been fundamental to my growth.

The shift took years, but with each 'NO' I said in order to live my own life on my own terms, I was moving closer to honoring myself. Putting *me* first became one of my biggest lessons. I learnt to start using my instincts as a guide. I learnt to check in with myself to see how I felt about a situation I was unsure about. I learnt to develop a relationship with my intuition and that was my biggest guide in knowing what was right or wrong. The woman I am today comes from a place of learning how to feel, and comprehend, when I am being valued or devalued and how to respond in each situation.

Big Mama was one woman who was very bold in expressing how she felt and was very comfortable with speaking her mind. When I was navigating my journey as a rape survivor and learning about boundaries, I was reflecting on the fine qualities Big Mama possessed. She would speak her mind and not shy away from what she had to say or what she felt she deserved. She knew where she stood and she taught me how to redefine my self-worth by owning my opinions. This lesson has been an invaluable tool for me as I move through life determined not to be defined by my past. By speaking up for what she believed in, my grandma taught me that redefining and constantly reassessing our values as human beings is the fundamental key to growth and a clear mindset.

I can now see that I was the victim of manipulation and abuse at the hands of my father, someone I was supposed to trust and feel safe with. As a child, and as most children do, I did whatever I could to cope and get myself through. As an adult, there came a moment when, if I wanted to truly experience closeness and happiness, I could no longer turn and look the other way. The 'trap' of coercion and control I found myself in was released when I saw these events for what they really were, but most importantly when I allowed my emotions, which had been stifled for so long, to have their freedom.

Faith

"Faith is taking the first step even when you don't see the whole staircase."

— **Martin Luthur King, Jr.**

When I was a child, Big Mama used to take me to the Hindu *Mandir* (temple), which was across the street from where we lived. She went religiously every Monday afternoon and on holidays I would go with her. I vividly remember the satsang (sacred gathering) she would attend. The attendees were mainly elderly women and I was usually the only child. Big Mama seemed proud that I was an obedient and religious granddaughter. I would feel a sense of warmth inside at the attention I got from all the elderly women. My grandmother was well liked in the community. More often than not, she would be on the receiving end of praise. I could hear them speaking to each other about how my grandma was able to convince her granddaughter – me – to attend prayers with her every Monday, since most of the other children wouldn't attend without a fight. The singing and Hindu prayers were not something most children would prefer to listen to. I did it to please Big Mama and the attention was an added bonus.

Once when we were getting ready to go to the Mandir, she told me that she wanted me to sing a *bhajan* (devotional song). Big Mama had a great voice and would sing all the time. Even if there was no particular occasion for her to sing religious songs, she would burst out into bhajans. She would do this when she was engaged in mundane tasks. Big Mama, along with Bha and his family, were all very musically inclined. They excelled at singing, playing the *tabla* (a pair of small drums) and the harmonium (pump organ). She really wanted the best for me so wished me to develop these skills, too. From childhood, singing bhajans was something that was customary in our household.

We arrived at the Mandir and I was nervous. While I was confident I could sing, I was terrified of freezing or forgetting the words. This was in sharp contrast to Big Mama, who was generally confident and calm. She oozed a level of self-esteem that I could only dream of having.

Before we entered the Mandir, we were required to remove our shoes. Whether one enters a house or a Mandir, one should always leave the shoes outside. Upon entering a holy place, Big Mama would touch the entrance of the floor with her fingers and place the same hand on her head. This action symbolizes that the ground is sacred and holy, and is a sign of respect and humility.

The hall was lined with a red wine colored carpet and enormous marble statues of Gods and Goddesses. The huge statues were intricately painted and filled every corner of the hall. It had a vibrant but also calming atmosphere. I loved looking at *Jhulelal* (a Sindhi deity) in the temple because our house was also covered with his framed pictures. Jhulelal has a majestic look with his golden crown and peacock feathers on top of it. He sits cross-legged on a fish, holding a holy scripture in his hand. He has white beard, almost like Santa Claus, and the air of a kind, paternal figure.

Big Mama had a favorite spot in the temple where she would always sit and naturally I would sit next to her. It was customary for people to sit on the floor, unless they couldn't for any reason. After we sat down, she would take time to compose herself. She got herself into the right state of mind by closing her eyes and mouthing the mantra she frequently chanted. I watched her and followed along.

The satsang would start with prayers and then it would proceed with different ladies singing a bhajan. Big Mama usually sang because she had a beautiful and melancholic voice, and it was clear everyone appreciated it. When they would tell her to sing, she would look at me and sometimes indicate for me to sing as well. Big Mama always wanted me to stand out and she would constantly give me opportunities to shine in front of the local community. I would sing nervously, to start, but with her strong presence singing along with me, it always gave me the courage to continue. Big Mama always believed in me. She pushed me to sing regardless of how I performed. Her faith in me eventually boosted me to have faith in myself. She was my biggest cheerleader.

Big Mama had devotion to God like no one else I knew. I was always shadowing her, and her devotion to God was another quality I picked up. It has been one of the biggest gifts she has passed down to me.

Big Mama showed me not just how to perform rituals, but how to cultivate love and devotion. When she sang, it came from within, from her heart. In the same way that she bathed the little deity figurines at home, she did everything with love and dedication.

Faith isn't about religion as much as it is about connecting with your inner self or a source bigger than yourself. Today, I am Buddhist. My faith in my inner self, which today I view as the God within (Bodhichitta, the enlightened mind) is what anchors me when I go through the ups and downs of life. When I am overwhelmed, my faith reminds me that there is a purpose and reason to life. It reminds me that suffering passes and is indeed a part of existence. As long as I have faith, I realize the deeper meaning to everything. I understand life is about learning through the rough patches.

Faith also means to trust, to let go of doubts and to trust in the unknown. When Big Mama demanded that I sang, I feared that I would forget the words and embarrass us both. I also feared that the women at the Mandir would not enjoy the sound of my voice. By spending time with Big Mama, I realized that I'm not expected to always be perfect. I just needed to sing with my heart, and to love what I do. If I could do that, things would work out for the best.

When I was in my mid-20s, our family split up because my father chose his second family over us. My mom and I moved to live in Jakarta for 10 months. Meanwhile, my brother worked in Hong Kong, so he continued to live there. Living in Jakarta was difficult because we didn't have a place of our own. With a job that paid really low wages, it was impossible to rent an apartment. Besides, commuting through public transport other than taxis isn't safe in Jakarta, and owning a car or being able to afford taxis would add to the expenses. This made living there almost impossible, so my mother and I decided to move back to Hong Kong. It was an incredibly difficult decision because we didn't have much money, and had no place to stay in Hong Kong because my brother was living in a one-room flat. But we knew there was no other alternative. Before finalizing the plan to leave Jakarta, I rang Papa in Spain. I expressed how we were considering making the move back to Hong Kong. He gave me his blessing, which meant he wholeheartedly supported me in doing what I felt was right.

When I needed the reassurance to take a leap of faith, I was fortunate to have it. Papa was that support when I needed someone in my corner. He said to me, "it will be hard, but if this is what you want to do, Big Mama and I support you all the way." Simply hearing those words gave me a huge push to go ahead with my plan. I told my mom's family that we were leaving, we got our flights booked and off we went. From that point onwards, I never looked back. In hindsight, it was one of the best life decisions I have ever made. However, had it not been for the faith Papa had in me, I don't know if I would have ever made it on my own.

When we returned to Hong Kong, it was just my mom, my brother and myself. Growing up, my brother and I weren't particularly close. I knew I wanted to form a closer bond with him and I wanted to get to know him better. It took time and effort, like with any relationship. He was always more reserved with his emotions than I am. He didn't know what his role was within the family – unsure of whether he was a big brother or a father figure or both. He played both roles and did more than most brothers would do. When his business picked up, he provided far more for me than my father ever did. We would travel together as a family to places like Dubai, Phuket, and London. Whenever I needed anything, he always made sure that I had it. He went out of his way to show his love by showing support.

Having a brother who was like a father to me, filled a void. He was protective and a good provider; the roles he felt he ought to live by. Once, when I needed a laptop for university, he made sure I had one. He would drag me out to parties and dinners with him so I had a 'life' as he put it, outside of work and home.

My brother's caring nature restored my faith in men. If there was one thing I feared, it was people pulling away because that's what my father did. My father choosing his second family over us made me lose faith in a man's ability to stay loyal or committed. This notion was partially alleviated when my brother was there for me during our fragile times living as a broken family. Despite his imperfections, he was someone I could consistently rely on.

When I was 28, as a mature student studying for a Bachelor's degree, I felt out of place, and struggled a bit with the workload, but I knew I needed the qualification. In my second year, I had a module on phonetics and phonology that bored me to death. It is unlike me to give up and lose faith in what I could achieve, but I did. I remember spending days and nights on the final essay and feeling completely stuck. The deadline was one day away and I had no choice but to get it done somehow. I handed in an incomplete assignment, which would massively affect my grade and my overall GPA. The nerd in me felt humiliated, but my brain could not comprehend what the essay required and I eventually gave up. To my surprise, my lecturer, Ms. So, wrote an email explaining she didn't want to fail me and what I'd handed in would result in a fail. She offered the chance to take my assignment back and redo it.

I was speechless. The first thing I asked myself was, "why does she care?" I had accepted what I was going to get and yet, for some reason, *she* didn't want to accept the poor quality of what I had done. My lecturer refused to give up on me, when I was ready to give up on myself. I was feeling the echo of what I experienced so many years earlier when Ms. Dobbs went out of her way to show she cared, even though Ms. So didn't know me very well. We had never connected on a personal level so to her, I thought I must have just been another undergraduate student.

When I went back to university to pick up my assignment, for some unknown reason, I felt braver and willing to fight. I didn't understand the assignment, let alone the course, and felt like I was hitting my head against a brick wall. Despite my frustration, being given a second chance gave me the opportunity to buckle down and try again. I worked day and night, rereading the module notes and handouts in their entirety, desperate for *something* to sink in. I reached out to my buddy for help and, before I knew it, I managed to complete the assignment. I handed it in gingerly – I was so uncertain about how I had done. Within a few days, Ms. So let me know that I had passed!

The moment Ms. So gave me a second chance, I remembered how much obtaining a degree with honors meant to me. I realized that when it got difficult, I had caved in and collapsed in the face of my perceived inadequacy. I learned from this experience that faith is what I'm supposed to fall back on when things get hard, not when they are easy! When everything is going according to plan, faith isn't needed. I realized that Ms. So reminded me of the very lesson that I had overlooked – to turn within, to trust in the process even when I couldn't see the whole staircase. It reminded me that all I needed to do was to take the first step and then the next, and not worry about where it would lead me. Faith and trust go hand-in-hand.

Believing in the goodness in people, as simple as it sounds, has a lot to do with faith. For as long as I can remember, I have always had an optimistic view about people in general, even when things weren't going my way. It helped that I had people around me who had faith in me or were there for me to lean on. It reinforced the very idea that goodness exists, which in return encouraged me to be an even better person.

The concept of 'goodness' is a big part of Buddhism because being good isn't about the actions you perform, but the person you are. It is about being humble, having mutual respect, having compassion for others' suffering and being kind. These values help me keep myself in check when I feel I've strayed.

A few years ago, I came back home from work, exhausted. The moment I walked in, I noticed that the kitchen was a complete mess. The clutter made me feel uncomfortable and agitated. In my opinion, a tidy kitchen makes a huge difference when preparing and cooking a meal. That evening, my (domestic) helper had been in so I was happily going home to what I thought would be a spotless kitchen. I proceeded to walk into the kitchen and I saw a lot of things were out of place.

Without filtering my reaction, I questioned my husband. I felt a great sense of annoyance as I frantically rushed to clean the kitchen. The 'messy' kitchen threw me off and brought out an unkind and irrational side in me. To cool my temper down, my husband hurriedly went back to the kitchen to sort out what he didn't see as catastrophic. He frantically moved objects around, uncertain as to why I was so annoyed.

The messy kitchen was a problem for me and I could have said something to my husband calmly, but I didn't and I ruined a perfectly nice evening. Besides spoiling our night, I felt I was in the right and I had no compassion when I spoke. Faith is remembering we still love the person even when a situation isn't pleasant. When we allow ourselves for a moment to forget, or we sound rude or impolite, love doesn't come through, only judgment does. I didn't bother to greet him as I walked through the door and instead of being loving and calm, I had a go at him. My personal values of seeing the good in him were thrown out the window.

This incident has taught me to be connected with who I am, especially when my reactions get the better of me. I still like my kitchen neat and tidy, but I am kinder when it isn't. When there are tea stains on the kitchen counter, I simply wipe the counter and sit and enjoy the delicious cup of cardamom tea my husband makes for me every day. I have learnt not to sweat the small stuff anymore.

One evening, I attended a Buddhist class at the *Kadampa* center and Gen Rabten (my Buddhist teacher) shared a story, which made me question my faith. A lady he knows in Australia, who is a Buddhist and attends the Kadampa classes, was going through some trauma in her life and he decided to check up on her. I'll name this lady Ann. She had a cancerous tumor, and was going through chemotherapy. Her husband had a heart condition. Her kids were going through a lot in school and were also coping with their ill parents. They both were aware that time was not on their side. Prior to his heart failure, her husband had a very good job. They had all life's luxuries, including houses in various places and two lovely children. When Rabten saw her during his visit to Australia, he asked her how she was doing. She responded by saying, "I can't imagine something really bad happening."

Puzzled by what she said, Rabten asked her to explain what she meant. She said, "I can't imagine losing my faith, my inner peace, or my Buddha."

When I heard Ann's perspective on her life situation, I was amazed because here was a married woman with children who was not only going through cancer, but she had a sick husband and they seemed about to lose everything. Yet, she was in a state of complete control of her emotions. Nothing fazed her and she was content with her life. I was awestruck at her depth of faith, and also envious because I wanted to have a mind like hers. Life does throw us curveballs. I wanted to be able to have that level of equilibrium, despite my world going crazy. Hearing that, I realized I had a lot of inner work to do. I needed to work on understanding the concept that to live means to go through ups and downs and the knowledge that while I'm undergoing a down phase, I need to check in with my inner self. I often ask myself "Is my mind calm despite the tough time or is it in pain, reacting to the situation?" Ann's way of living through her own turmoil was a reminder of how I want to live.

For people like me, who've gone through childhood trauma, one of the consequences is to want to control the things you can control, especially since you couldn't have control over what happened to you as a child. I now know there is a source of power or strength beyond myself, and when I go into 'control mode' it is because deep down I fear that things might not pan out the way I want them to. I then lose my sense of faith in what is meant to be. When I feel like this, I remind myself of the Beatles song 'Let it Be,' and it reminds me to trust in the flow of life.

Compassion

"Until one has loved an animal, a part of one's soul remains unawakened."

— **Anatole France**

When I was a child, I genuinely enjoyed eating chicken and seafood. I didn't even think about the meat as having once been a living thing. Animals were never really on my radar and I didn't consider their physical or emotional wellbeing. In my family, Sindhi rituals were regularly enacted. One such tradition was eating seafood on Fridays because the Sindhi (people originally from Sindh) deity Jhulelal resides in the sea.

Jhulelal is revered as the God of the sea for Sindhis, and we hear legends abound about the miracles and birth of Jhulelal. In the 10th century A.D., the ruler at the time, Mirk Shah, demanded that the Sindhi Hindus in the region convert to Islam. Shocked at this, the Sindhis prayed for 40 days solid by the sea. Jhulelal is said to be the savior who was born on the 40th day. In adulthood, Jhulelal was arrested for speaking up and suggesting that religion originates from one source. This concept was received with a great deal of apprehension and he was arrested. Finally, the day came for the trial. While the trial was taking place, water gushed into the courtroom and many people drowned. Then it was said that a fire appeared out of nowhere. Mirk Shah was understandably scared and asked for mercy. Mercy was given and everything returned back to the state it was before this incident. Sindhis no longer had to convert to Islam and a relative peace was proclaimed between the two groups. Jhulelal was then worshipped by his people until his death and to this day people worship his connection to the sea.

Today this doesn't make any sense to me because if I worshipped the sea, then I would protect it by not eating sea creatures. How can fishing, killing and eating living beings be justified in the name of religion? But up until the last few years, I had given it little thought. If we get something put in front of us as a kid then we eat it. If our parents think it is good, then in turn it must be good; as how could they be wrong? I was clearly ignorant about the concept of what animals are from a very young age. Upon reflection, I started to question what I was doing when I was consuming meat. Was it a good act? Was it making the world a better place? Was it good for the environment?

*   *   *

My father had a store on the second floor of a dilapidated building, and he would often bring me with him when he worked there. Once, when I was desperate for the toilet, I had to walk around the corner to the dark, moldy side of the building where the run-down toilet was located. The toilet was always damp, humid and congested with rotting refuse from other people. The smell of old, putrid excrement always hung in the toilet and the corridors around. The faeces covered flush never worked and there was a lack of useable toilet paper. Excrement was sometimes smeared on the walls with little pieces of paper attached and flies and roaches lived there in abundance. It was the kind of place where you held your breath when you entered. The taps often didn't work. Good luck trying to wash your hands!

Every single time I needed to relieve myself, I would encounter a stray tabby cat. Why it was attracted to that place, I'm not sure. She had piercing eyes that stared at me, causing shivers to run up and down my spine. When I saw her, I was terrified because her eyes looked unwelcoming and judgmental. She just stared at me, silently watching. I felt strongly that she didn't like me. She could probably smell the fear and apprehension I exuded whenever in her presence.

The cat held a lot of power over me during those years. I was always scared that she might suddenly lunge at me, claw or bite me, even though she had never done any of these things. Upon seeing her, my anxiety level would rise and I'd begin to think less rationally. All I saw was a small, rabid creature that was waiting to attack ME. Every time I would reluctantly visit her domain, she lay in wait, like a monster at the bottom of the bed. More often than not, fear would turn me in the other direction and I would find myself walking back the way I came. I had to be really desperate to risk spending time with that cat!

I didn't like her and didn't like animals in general. I didn't understand why they were allowed to be in our environment. Living in the city, I became detached from the idea and experience of animals. Compassion or empathy for nature wasn't something I was exposed to and so, by default, they never crossed my mind. Insects and animals were completely foreign to me. Nothing made me want to seek them out or respect them. It does make me wonder what I was told by my parents as a child that made me so frightened of animals. I don't remember having any negative experiences – except with the tabby cat – and yet I was immensely apprehensive in their presence.

I couldn't be more different today. Animals have helped me to appreciate much more about the world that we live in and helped me understand who I want to become. I have gained more knowledge about compassion since being vegan than all the years of education I underwent. I can't actually ever remember learning about animals and insects in class! Some animals have shown me how to embody some of life's essential qualities. Dogs have shown me what loyalty and kindness mean and cats have shown me the true meaning of calm. I can clearly see animals have so much more to teach me. To witness their suffering head-on, when my heart ached and I felt their pain, assisted me in expanding my empathy radar. Each experience I have had, looking at life through the eyes of animals has taught me that they know compassion far more than we often do as humans.

I know that animals instinctively hunt for food, which does involve killing other species. But I have also seen another more compassionate side to animals, especially from those that have been domesticated. It seems that they have the ability to be far more kind-hearted and empathetic than we do. We, as a species, have evolved far beyond being hunter gatherers and yet we continue to slaughter animals in a similar way to the way our ancestors did. In my opinion, the evolution of our intelligence hasn't progressed at the same rate as our compassion. We are so engrossed in our own wants and needs that we do not truly desire to know about other people's suffering, let alone the suffering of animals. We choose to turn a blind eye because it is simply easier that way, and by doing so it often enables us to obtain what we want for ourselves in life. How many people walk by homeless people in the street without a second thought? Many people live life thinking only about themselves and use reason to justify their actions, believing that inherent selfishness will lead to success. Invariably, I have seen many instances where that does appear to be the case; as the world does reward selfishness, drive and individualism. I often wonder when are we going to realize that this shouldn't just be about self and other, and that we are all part of the same interlinked ecosystem?

Every Sunday, our family would have regular meals out to bond with each other and enjoy the evening together. Korean food was one of my favorite cuisines, and I would always feel a sense of excitement in my heart whenever I got to choose my favorite Korean restaurant. The smell of marinated raw meat placed on the table in front of us didn't faze me. For me it was meat, not an animal. My father and I would take turns to barbeque and wait for everyone to comment on who was the better chef. Funnily enough, the meat was already seasoned and our skills were measured by who could cook the tenderest piece of meat without burning it. If Big Mama knew, she might have been proud that I had the skills in me to cook, even at such a young age.

When I was 17, something clicked within me and I became vegetarian. As a teenager, I was constantly seeking role models and new values to follow so I could become a better person. Although I knew animals were tortured and killed, I had no idea to what extent. I consciously wanted to change to be a more compassionate human being and made the steps necessary to make this transition. The lectures in the temple helped, as did Big Mama, who helped me reassess and consider what I was eating. As far as I know, Big Mama had been a vegetarian her entire life.

Initially, when social gatherings occurred, I felt somewhat isolated. On some occasions, I put others needs before my own because I didn't know how to speak up and make it clear that I was a vegetarian. This was a recurring theme for me and I often felt like the odd one out. Unfortunately, the host would often forget that I was vegetarian and serve me meat. Then would come that awkward conversation. I found myself continuously having to defend my lifestyle choices and the focus of the gathering would be on me and my 'unusual' eating habits. I would answer their incredulous questions politely, while inwardly thinking that if people really knew what they were consuming and saw the way animals were treated, most would change their ways.

Big Mama was a 'pure' vegetarian (no meat or eggs, but consumed dairy), and she was secure in living with that choice. However, Papa was happy to be an omnivore. Despite this, Big Mama had no qualms about cooking chicken or fish for him. My aunt (Big Mama's daughter-in-law) is a vegetarian and it became normal, and somewhat expected, for the ladies of the family to eventually become vegetarian. It was very normal also for some of the men in the family to be vegetarian. Bha and two out of his three sons switched and became vegetarian as well.

In my late-20s, something strange happened that resulted in me deciding to drop vegetarianism. I'm not quite sure what was going through my mind at the time. Suddenly, I had a hunger for fish and this craving was unrelenting. I didn't think twice about the fact that this craving should be sated. In hindsight, I realized I gave in to the first fleeting thought I had, which was unusual as I am usually more careful in my decision-making. The temptation and my perceived need to eat fish was far greater than my compassion for animals.

My love for animals wasn't deeply rooted enough at that time in my life. Being vegetarian felt inconvenient and I was ashamed of being different than people in my social circle. I even found it difficult when I went on dates. Whenever the menu came out I always had to mention that I was vegetarian, which would inevitably lead to that conversation again. Many men I dated found it funny and just thought I was an oddity. I would get asked if I would touch meat. Would I cook meat? What about the smell? Would I make my children be vegetarian? I found the series of questions always the same and unrelenting. I know from speaking to other vegetarians (or pescatarians like my husband) that this has always been a recurring theme for them also. Certainly they have been laughed at, ridiculed and mocked for refusing to eat cows, sheep, birds, pigs and other animals. I had to continuously stand up for my ideologies and my arguments for not eating meat, which were never respected or accepted. I decided that I wasn't brave enough to be that person, at least not yet. Thinking about eating fish and meat shook my already shaky conviction. I imagined what it would be like to tuck into a burger. I envisioned the warm explosion of taste in the mouth at the first bite. I suddenly realized that my reasons for being vegetarian were not on solid ground. I felt this desire seed in my mind and I knew that at some point in the future I was likely to give in.

One random morning I got up and told my brother that I wanted a Filet-O-Fish from McDonald's. Initially, he thought I was joking and dismissed my statement. But on this occasion, I was deadly serious. I'd dreamed about eating a Filet O-fish the night before and all I could think about was McDonald's. I pictured holding the burger in my two hands and raising it slowly to my lips. I visualized myself taking that first bite, watching the tartar sauce gently ease from the burger into my mouth and onto my tongue. I could taste the warmth of the moist fish within my mouth as I took bite after bite. I could imagine the smell and nothing was going to stop me.

He turned to me and stated categorically, "I'll go get you one, but then you will have to eat it." I agreed to his mini-challenge. When he came home, the wrapped up burger was presented to me. My brother held it in front of me with a wide grin, challenging me to eat it. He uttered four simple words "Here you go, Komie." I looked eagerly at the burger and the familiar aroma clouded my judgment.

"Eat it Komie," he said again as he glanced at me, somewhat confused by my unexpected craving for the fish burger. He moved it closer to my face. I took the burger from his hand and ate it with fervor as if it was a test. I needed to prove to myself that I fitted in; that I was like the majority – the omnivores, the normal people, the strong people in my life. As I swallowed morsel after morsel of that burger, the values I held were stripped away from me. I became one of the masses who love devouring animal flesh. Something deep inside me knew that what I was doing was wrong, but I did it anyway. I felt part of the greater whole. There would be no more discussions about vegetarianism, no more time spent on defending my beliefs and values. And certainly no more opportunities for ridicule. I could be normal again. So, for the next 10 years I was an omnivore, and I allowed myself to eat whatever I wanted.

*   *   *

About five years ago, I started experimenting with different diets suggested by the gym where I was training. Both Keto and Paleo are commonly followed diets for quick weight loss. Both diets eliminate grains, legumes and sugar. They also encourage eating healthy fats (nuts, seeds and animal fat), animal protein and leafy greens. Within a Paleo diet there are no restrictions on how many starchy vegetables or fruits you can consume. However, Keto diets also measure fat, protein and carb intake. Keto is stricter regarding carb intake and promotes a higher percentage of fat consumption. At that time in my life I was driven to lose weight, so I adopted the Keto plan. It worked wonders for me, for a while, because I finally had abs! To have rock hard abs was an accomplishment for me, as it meant that I was strong and fit. As a kid, I never felt particularly resilient and didn't partake in fitness or exercise. Having abs made me feel great, at least for a while.

I was consciously reinventing who I was and eager to change my sense of identity. Exercise, as well as my diet, assisted in this systematic transformation. While I enjoyed having a toned physique, I also developed an unhealthy obsession with abdominal muscles. In my earlier years, my stomach used to stick out and that troubled me. Seeing the results of my transformation in the mirror, I felt like a new me. As I trained even harder and more regularly, I saw more change and definition, which motivated me even more. I became a gymaholic. However, my new look didn't last long. Suddenly, I noticed strange aches in my stomach after meals.

The pain would be excruciatingly intense, and would leave me close to tears. Bloated and uncomfortable, I pondered about the root cause of the ache in my stomach. I started to feel greater levels of discomfort and pain; and I watched as my dream body faded into the distance. Gradually all the hard work over many years began to evaporate right in front of my eyes. Eventually, I began to experience debilitating pain that rendered me bedridden and unable to do very much except think about the pain. Obviously, I wasn't able to go to the gym. When I did try going, I found it impossible to be mindful of any exercise I was doing.

Out of frustration, I tried to continue to make changes that might make a difference. I started adding fiber powder to my breakfast and consciously included more water in my daily routine. I made sure I was regularly taking vitamin tablets and went to bed early so I had enough sleep. None of this helped and I saw that my stomach was only getting worse. I even went as far as resorting to Reiki; but nothing came of that. I wasn't getting any better and my stomach continued to grow at a ridiculous rate. I became constipated and my stomach was bloated for weeks. My strong and toned physique had dissipated into a flabby, unrecognizable mess. After nearly two months of pain and constipation, I decided to finally seek medical assistance. I went to get a colonoscopy and a gastroscopy because I couldn't cope with the situation anymore!

I was under anesthesia during the whole procedure, which took a little less than an hour. I got up feeling groggy and disoriented as a result of the drug. I took a deep breath and looked around me. The examination room reminded me of the changes in my lifestyle once again. Why was I here? And how on Earth had I ended up here? I finally managed to get dressed and see the doctor for my results. While I was nervous and shaking, the doctor told me everything was fine. I found myself feeling frustrated and angry. How could I be 'fine' when I was feeling so unwell? I felt more frustrated than ever before. I left the doctor, angry, confused and feeling more than a little defeated.

Out of sheer desperation, I went to see my GP and told him about my stomach problem. He prescribed oral medication and suppositories. I found out that I had classic symptoms of IBS (Irritable Bowel Syndrome). I needed to understand the implications of severe IBS so I did research on the subject as well as asking people around me.

The Mayo Clinic states that IBS is a common disorder that affects the colon as the main function of the colon is to absorb water and nutrients from food that has been digested. Symptoms can include abdominal pain, diarrhea or constipation, bloating and gas. I was dumbstruck. Confusion started to play games in my brain. How can all of these symptoms be associated with one disorder, considering that constipation and diarrhea are on two opposite sides of the spectrum? I decided that the only way forward was to heal my body with proper diet and exercise.

When I was stuck and felt as if nothing was going to work, I came up with a new plan of action. I decided to eliminate meat and eggs from my diet and see how it would pan out. I added oats and more *pak choy*, which is a Chinese cabbage that has leafy greens with white stems; *choi sum*, also a Chinese green flowering cabbage with edible tiny yellow flowers; and a variety of fruits, lentils and rice. I stuck to this diet for a few weeks and gradually started to notice some significant changes. I began to have regular bowel movements; and I found that the swelling in my stomach reduced. Over time, my body returned to a healthier weight and I progressively started to bring back other fruits and vegetables. Though the diet seemed dull, it was clearly showing me results. As time went on, I increasingly felt better about my body and the pain steadily diminished. Addressing what I was eating paved the way to a healthier lifestyle.

At around this time, my Form Six (Grade 12) students were preparing for their Individual Oral Presentation assessments on a variety of different social issues. A number of my students chose topics on animal cruelty and social injustice. I was definitely moved by their allocutions as they came up with some points that I hadn't heard before. Their presentations must have been powerful: they inspired me to start researching animal ethics and why we consume meat. I began reading books on animal rights by Peter Singer and started to address what this meant to me. Typically, we are told, especially by the fitness industry, that protein equates to meat.

This belief that protein comes solely from animals and that we need to consume an abundance to retain muscle mass has been propagated by the majority of people, and I had fallen for it too! I was so hooked on getting fit and having a better physique that I hadn't considered the immense suffering I was also creating. While protein is important, I learnt that it doesn't just come from meat! Vegetables, tempeh, tofu and legumes are high in protein, too. But over the years, the shoddy protein argument seems to have been used as the main logic as to why we should eat meat. I felt a great sense of guilt as I realized I was also responsible for forwarding this very weak argument to others. At one point, I had even tried to get my husband to eat meat, but to his credit, he remained disinterested.

I started watching documentaries like *Cowspiracy, Forks Over Knives,* and *Earthlings.* I was shocked and mortified by how little I knew about animal agriculture. I was heartbroken and horrified to witness animals being slaughtered in such a horrific manner. It was much worse than any horror movie you could ever watch. The conditions in which pigs, cows, and chickens were living showed me that they were not cared for at all. No horror movie could be as scary as what was happening in reality to those animals. But what we don't see we don't think about.

In one of the videos, pigs were crammed in together, screaming for mercy, waiting to be slaughtered. It was a dark, crappy area where you could see nothing but pigs forced into a tight space. Blood was splattered everywhere, though it was hard to see in the semi-darkness. Fear and confusion filled their eyes. I looked on as their throats were being repeatedly slit until they were dead. There was one baby pig that wanted to be with his family, he just wanted to live. He clearly had no idea why there was so much death and violence around him. He was just a baby piglet and he was hearing other pigs crying with screams of pain. He heard his fellow pigs begging to be left free, fighting for their lives. Before he knew it, his own throat was cut wide open, his life selfishly ripped from him for no other reason than food. One at a time, each pig went through the same brutal experience. Society calls it butchery or animal agriculture. I call it murder. And the worst thing is I was once accepting of this slaughter and the people who partake in it. Not anymore. It is about time that we as a collective species stand up and take responsibility for what is happening. How can we claim that we love animals and yet allow some to suffer in such a cruel manner?

In another video a baby cow was lying on the ground. She reminded me of a pile of rubbish, as if her life meant nothing at all. She was clearly ready to be used. Because of our greed and inherent selfishness; she was killed without any mercy, without any thought. Her life was robbed of her flesh for food and her skin for us to use as leather. Within minutes, the calf was rendered insignificant. She didn't have a say in her own life and no one stood up to protect her. I was in agony knowing all this, and that most people have no idea that this is going on behind closed doors. Or they do know and they choose to do nothing, which for me is even more deeply disturbing. If they choose to do nothing, what does it tell us about their moral fiber? Surely a good person would do something about this?

After watching the documentaries and reflecting on what I had seen, I gave up eating meat for good. There was no way I could continue walking on that path with a clear conscience. Beforehand, buying meat produce from the supermarket enabled me to never see it for what it really is. I'd usually buy chicken breast, turkey burgers, or salmon steaks wrapped up in convenient plastic packaging so I didn't stop to ponder where it all actually came from. It didn't cross my mind what it really was and I didn't think much about it. I was too busy with other 'more important' life matters. Meanwhile, I continued to finance the slaughter. I was clearly fine living in blissful ignorance of the food I was consuming. I never really considered how a chicken breast landed on my plate, until clear evidence about slaughterhouses was presented to me. How could I claim to be compassionate, kind and good when I continued to eat meat and how could I claim to love animals and nature?

I thought it was going to be difficult to make the switch to veganism, but I wanted to make that necessary shift. Vegetarianism was still a good step but it was not enough for me, especially after what I had seen. Most people don't realize just how much violence and cruelty underpins the dairy and egg industries, so I wanted to be free from them, too. I wanted to make the leap to a diet that was compassionate to animals, and one that shows respect for the environment. I didn't want to be even partly responsible for any of that suffering. To my surprise, the shift from omnivore to vegan was actually quite easy. I slowly replaced my omnivore breakfast of fluffy scrambled eggs alongside onion, tomatoes and smoked salmon, with berries on rice milk oats and toast with creamy avocado. One of the things I noticed was that I felt noticeably lighter from eating vegan food. Eggs generally made me feel heavy and fuller, but it was also harder for my stomach to digest. It took me a long time to enjoy eating oats because I didn't like any form of cereal, even as a kid. Toast with butter was my favorite breakfast option as a child, and oats reminded me of old people's food as Big Mama would eat them as a warm morning treat. Through the years, oats have become my breakfast of champions, as Big Mama's DNA resonates through me as I am more compassionate about what I put into my body.

* * *

I used to live in Discovery Bay, a small community on the island of Lantau on the southwest side of Hong Kong. I came across dogs, birds, fish and turtles, which I never saw living in the congested city as a young girl. Weekend routines on the island include walks around the natural parks with my husband to feed the fish and turtles, while soaking in the fresh breeze from the bay.

One day, on our usual stroll, I noticed a bird – a red-whiskered bulbul on a tree branch. He was perched all alone, examining the world around him with small movements of his head. He was white and black with a grey body and he had a pointy tip like a triangle on his head. His eyes were a beautiful combination of white and black. He had a bright red spot right beside his eyes. I adored looking at the array of colors decorated on his tiny yet majestic body. I remembered thinking that he was an intelligent fellow because, whenever we threw some breadcrumbs high up into the sky, he would fly and grab them in mid-air. It was such a delight to watch. Suddenly, I had tears in my eyes. I started confessing all my sins. I stood there, crying as I told him how sorry I was for eating his relatives (chickens and turkeys) and how I was aware that my apology would not bring them back to life. It was heart wrenching to realize I had done this to them as I locked eyes with that bird. A deep sense of regret and pain consumed me, which I had not experienced before. I felt like I had committed terrible sins and felt a deep and overwhelming sense of grief. I found myself weeping like a child. I could actually feel my heart hurt with every breath that I took. I continued explaining to the bird between sobs how humans don't deserve this planet because clearly we are so caught up in our selfishness. We fail to see anything other than our own wants and desires. I promised the bird that I would do whatever I could to bring more awareness to society. This may sound crazy to most people because I was talking to a bird, but don't we talk to our dogs, cats or babies this way? Today, I see no fundamental differences between all living animals. It was on that day that I found peace and confirmation that we all are connected; our bodies are different but we all are living creatures with a heart, mind and soul.

Four years ago, my husband and I were in Yangon on holiday. As we walked out of the hotel, we saw a dead rat spattered on the side of the road, with blood sprayed all over and next to its tiny, lifeless body. Its corpse just lay there for all to see. In the past, I wouldn't have noticed it let alone stopped to see if it was breathing. At first, I questioned the cause of how it died. But regardless of how it happened, I noticed that I was in pain. I felt for the life of this now dead being. The fact that nobody seemed to notice this innocent creature's body on the street spiked my empathy radar again. Thoughts of how cruel and numb our society has become started to infiltrate my mind.

This incident – although mundane to some – shook me. I witnessed a small part of suffering, but I was beside myself with grief. When I saw the grey mangled rat lying on the street dead, and how a number of passersby ignored him, a lesson was presented in front of me that day. We can be cruel to one another, and all I wanted was to believe that all living things should be given an equal chance, despite size, shape, color, gender or species.

Back at my hotel room, still frozen from the incident, I collected my thoughts, sat down and messaged my Buddhist teacher, Gen Rabten, telling him what I witnessed and how I felt. He explained that what I was experiencing was a window to empathy. I was starting to feel compassion and love for creatures. He believed that my thoughts on becoming vegan were an opening towards reconstructing my feelings, and deep empathy, towards animals, which I had not experienced until that day.

*   *   *

Cooking vegan meals has transported me into a new and alien world. Preparing and shopping for food became more difficult as I learned to be more conscientious about checking the labels and packaging. It was a steep learning curve, and as I learned more, it equipped me with information to help me decipher what to buy and what to avoid. The vegan community in general is very good at sharing information and supporting each other.

Some people find the whole idea of what is and isn't vegan food difficult. For example, some bread isn't vegan. I understand their frustration because foods like bread can easily be vegan. The problem is that many people aren't familiar with veganism like they are with vegetarianism. Lack of information about veganism in general creates these issues. About a year ago, I was looking for vegan protein powder and the distributor was persuading me to buy a particular brand, saying it is the best protein powder in the fitness industry. I kept repeating to her "I'm vegan, and this powder has whey in it, which is derived from milk." She couldn't comprehend and continued to sell the product to me despite it not being vegan. Whey comes in a powder form and, therefore, may not initially look like an animal product. For many people, "invisible" animal products such as casein, whey, or gelatin seem irrelevant. Most people also don't realize that honey isn't vegan. The difficulty is that dairy or extracts of animal fat or bone can be found in a range of different foods, including biscuits, cookies, chocolates and even gummy bears. When visiting family or friends, this can be awkward to explain because the meat or bone is not visible to the naked eye. It involves a whole new way of thinking about food and its ingredients.

At first, I found dining out very difficult. I realized that that I needed to research restaurants prior to the meal to check on their food choices. Otherwise I often end up eating next to nothing, which has happened several times. However, there are a good variety of vegan restaurants in Hong Kong and I'm now comfortable suggesting dining at a vegan restaurant with friends. They too get a chance to see what vegan food tastes like, and some of them enjoy the experience. Three years into my newfound diet, I'm more at ease about being clear on what I will and will not eat. I'm also ready to stick up for my values, beliefs and ethical standards. I refuse to go back to my days of weaker conviction and cower on the side eating bread with olive oil as a meal. Picking a venue and having a say in where we go for social gatherings with my friends has made it much easier for me to venture out and socialize without being ostracized.

Recently, my former assistant principal remembered it was my birthday and bought me a cake. I was touched, but I couldn't eat it because it contained animal products so I gave it to my colleague. She later learnt that I am a vegan and felt terrible. I had to explain how happy I was that she remembered me on my special day and that the cake in itself didn't matter as much because the gesture was heartfelt. My students also heard about my birthday and went out of their way to get me a vegan pudding, which was so thoughtful and touching! I'm enamored and heartened by people around me who are interested in learning about veganism, and I hold the hope they will experiment with or adopt this lifestyle as they research and see the countless benefits it brings to one's health, environment, and to animals. In my deepest heart of hearts, I desire to see people embody caring and compassion and switch to a vegan diet. It will happen one day – when people connect the dots and truly understand that the lives of animals do matter. By simply changing our diet, we have the chance to save our planet. Changing what we eat is a small sacrifice for the future of this world and for the millions of animals that will be saved.

Every day, I bring my packed lunch to school. On one occasion, I brought *banh mi*, which is a Vietnamese sandwich in a baguette. I used soya-minced 'meat' and cooked it with onions, garlic, curry powder, turmeric and sweet basil. I added sun-dried tomatoes and Daiya cheddar cheese onto the whole-wheat baguette, packed it up and took it to work. I noticed my colleague's eyes close as the aroma of my lunch tickled her nose and reached down to her taste buds. She was tempted to try so I gave her a little piece and she loved it. She said, "no wonder your husband is happy eating vegan food, this is so delicious!" Over time, by bringing more food to school, my colleagues are being introduced to alternative healthy vegan food choices. Although small and subtle transformations are happening around me with regard to veganism, it is clear that one step at a time is the way towards creating little ripples of change.

After I had sorted out my dietary requirements, I spent time researching animal cruelty in the cosmetic industry. I began looking at my own choices of makeup to see if they were vegan. PETA has a list on its website indicating which make up brands are tested on animals. I saw how animals continue are exploited in this industry and I felt the need to make that switch. Many brands, such as MAC, L'Oreal, Bobbi Brown, and a lot more, use rabbits or other animals for testing; especially if the products are being sold in China (which has mandatory animal testing!). When I realized the widespread exploitation of animals in this area, I began to look for alternatives. My mission was to find make-up brands in Hong Kong I could purchase, which were free from animal cruelty.

When my concealer and foundation ran out, I made the switch and now use Glass Hour. By chance I have always used Bella Pierre and it has a vegan line of loose foundation, lip-gloss, eyeliner, blush, and so much more. Being ethically vegan means not using any products that contain animals/

insects or have been tested on animals/insects. Even now, I have yet to find a vegan friendly clothing line that is reasonable and durable. When I need a replacement, I will shop online; PETA has a list of vegan clothing stores so that is usually my go-to for clothes shopping.

*   *   *

Last December, when Big Mama was in critical condition, I flew to Barcelona where she was living with my relatives. It was the first time I had seen them since turning vegan, so there were many foods that I was given that I couldn't eat. In an Indian household many use *ghee*, which is clarified butter. They don't cook with *ghee*, but milk and other dairy products were definitely a problem because I was the only vegan in the house. Meals had to be adjusted to accommodate my dietary requirements. I was uncomfortable with causing inconvenience to them because they had to alter ingredients in some dishes and that can be difficult for those who aren't familiar with vegan cooking. Indian cooking is ladled with cream, milk, yoghurt, butter and paneer, which is cottage cheese. I appreciated the fact that they would constantly ask and work around my dietary needs, which showed me that they cared. However, there were occasions veganism was an issue. On one such occasion, I joined everyone in the living room, where they were waiting to indulge in a delicious-looking chocolate Christmas log cake. I had to politely decline and made it clear that I couldn't eat it. Confused, they asked why I wouldn't eat the Christmas cake that they had taken ages making. I felt a great sense of guilt but I still would not eat the cake. My ethical standard may have seemed rigid and without intention I seemed to have spoiled things for them. The atmosphere markedly changed.

In the past Big Mama used to make *prasad*, religious food offerings such as *karao*, which is made of whole-wheat flour, sugar and butter (veganism isn't big in India or among Hindu communities). She rejoiced in the preparation of stirring the concoction until the entire kitchen smelled like sweet buttery candy. Big Mama was filled with love in performing this ritual that is commonly practiced by Hindus. *Karao* is made on special days, based on the Sindhi calendar, which is strictly followed in our family. Big Mama would chant the Lord's name while preparing holy offerings. This became her practice with everything she cooked – figuratively dedicating the food to God, which meant the food too was filled with love and compassion. As Big Mama got older, she chanted the Lord's name regardless of what she was doing. You could literally feel love and compassion radiating through her. After her passing, I realized that she taught me about kindheartedness, empathy and love through her way of being. I will stay vegan for the rest of my life not just for the animals and the planet; but for her.

Mindful Living

"One of the advantages of being born in an affluent society is that if one has any intelligence at all, one will realize that having more and more won't solve the problem, and happiness does not lie in possessions, or even relationships: The answer lies within ourselves. If we can't find peace and happiness there, it's not going to come from the outside."

– Tenzin Palmo

One night, I saw Mama and Dad all dressed up in their formal wear. My brother and I were little; I was around six years old and my brother was nearly eight. Mama was wearing a royal blue, glittering sari with embroidery, fine sparkly diamond jewelry, and full make-up. In her cozy room, I had stood by her dressing table, watching her get dolled up. My innocent young eyes gazed at her magical transformation from a stay-at-home mom to a glamorous Indian beauty. To finish, she spritzed herself with a delicately scented perfume that was intoxicating to the point that I couldn't stop following her around. It reminded me of royalty.

Dad was wearing his fine black suit and a striking pink tie. They looked like Romeo and Juliet – or the Indian versions, at least – as they headed off to a *Diwali* ball, which is a celebration of the Indian New Year. Mama told me that she was wearing a new ring that my dad had given her for Diwali. She was glowing, as her well-manicured hand carried the diamond ring elegantly. The ring had intricate details: it was an attention-grabbing floral piece surrounded by glistening diamonds. It was bold yet delicate, and the small diamonds would shimmer when hit by the light. As a child, I saw my mom become happier when she received presents, especially from my dad that night when she was gifted with the possession of an exceptional diamond ring, the smile that radiated from her face was one of sheer joy. As a child, I was amazed at how such a tiny thing could convert her whole persona.

Gravitating towards people in the search for happiness seems like an automatic feature of the human psyche. We believe a relationship or marriage will bring us contentment and save us from a life of loneliness. As a child, I was glued to watching Hindi films, especially romantic ones, following the amazing journeys of my favorite actors and actresses. Most of these movies had one underlying message, and it was the value of the quest to live 'happily ever after,' while also highlighting how most of the girls weren't happy before they found love. Take *Bride and Prejudice* (the Indian version of Pride and Prejudice) as an example: the parents kept attending weddings and stressing about finding eligible suitors for their daughters to the point that it became a burden. They attended weddings and traveled across the world for that very reason – to find the right man. Luckily, their daughters found their Prince Charmings, but the message it creates is alarming. The girls aren't actually living until they are married. A girl's life starts after marriage. These movies, and my family, drilled this into me. Marriage was the unspoken rescue for the Indian girls who were destined to live a life with their in-laws, absorbed into another family. My family neglected to mention that the expectation of Indian women to marry into their husband's families meant, more often than not, that freedom was non-existent.

The night I saw them all dressed up for Diwali, I could see my mother playing the part of the blissful wife, overjoyed by a generous gift and ready to float off into their evening, gratefully clutching the arm of her spouse. If I had only ever seen them in that moment, I would have assumed they were the happiest of married couples, without a care in the world – I would have seen the fairytale. What I knew, though, was that there were more than just cracks in the façade.

*   *   *

I have noticed the tendency in people to attribute their happiness to possessions. In many cases, it could also be said that obtaining a husband or wife is just another prized 'possession' to accumulate. Certainly it seems this way when we watch the glamorous Bollywood movies, with an empty and wistful girl finding her 'completion' in the handsome man who acquires her. We are so afraid of experiencing a feeling of lack, or that we are not enough, that we turn to people and things to attempt to fill the holes in our lives.

I want to tell you about my friend. Let's call her Lisa. The iPhone 8 made its debut and Lisa has been thinking about it for weeks. She's been doing her research, asking friends and colleagues about it. Finally, she goes to the store to try it out and to see what the fuss is all about. Lisa suddenly feels a sense of euphoria and thinks the phone is the best gadget she has ever encountered, and this will somehow fill a void in her life. Led by her desire and obsession, she makes the new purchase. Once she has it, Lisa is on cloud nine and in love with her iPhone 8, until her friend, Zara, reveals to her that the Samsung Galaxy

S9 has some newer functions – more advanced than the iPhone 8 – that will blow her mind. Tempted, and feeling somewhat down that she didn't buy the Samsung instead of the iPhone, obsession kicks in again and she feels desperate, agonizing over whether she made the right choice. In my opinion, this is a formula destined for sheer unhappiness. It is clear that, with skillful marketing, fast-paced technological advances, and the feeling of wanting to belong, has catapulted our society towards valuing materialism over much else.

Possessions, unlike humans, are lifeless and yet we place immense regard on items when they are dear to us. The moment we decide an item isn't worth our time, it becomes redundant and we move on to something new. For some people, the way we treat our partner is no different to how we treat things; a new one is always better than the old. For some, the thought of a new lover is more exciting and more fun than the current one. Thus, we create for ourselves the waves of desire and euphoria all over again, with peaks and troughs similar to an addiction. We have failed to grasp what true happiness is and how it can be attained. We are searching for it in all the wrong places.

In my 20s, I had no direction as to where my life was going. I had no steady boyfriend and a job that didn't offer any meaning. At the same time, my friends were moving away and getting married, and I felt left behind. Shopping became one of my highlights and a source of comfort. In hindsight, I realize it was probably to fill the void of loneliness. I wasn't a shopaholic to the point of accumulating debt – luckily, I had my head screwed on right on that front – but, nevertheless, I spent money on luxury bags like Prada and Gucci and bought tons of pricey skincare products. Shopping became a hobby and it had become a normal activity for many in my community. We lived to work so that we could shop and purchase things to make us happier.

When I was 28 or 29, my brother bought me a gorgeous white-and-blue Prada shopping bag. It was one-of-a-kind, and it had an image of a Venetian gondola in clear azure blue waters. The blonde gondolier was wearing a striking red neckerchief and had a huge grin across his face. He looked as happy as I did. In the distance, there were blocks of low-rise buildings in beige with imperial red roofs. Looking at it was like being transported to Venice. The expensive bag took my breath away. But, over a period of time, the luxurious bag became less exciting to carry. I got accustomed to owning it and the thrill I initially had dissipated. The satisfaction I once had died down because I was wired to constantly want more, something better and new, to replace what I had. As a society, that is how humans operate; we get bored of what we have been longing for soon after we have purchased it. Trying desperately to keep up with the excitement by finding new items to buy becomes our next goal. This, I know now from experience, is a never-ending cycle of unattained happiness.

I soon learnt that my quest for external happiness seldom lasted. In my 30s, I followed the path to Buddhism, where I discovered there is an underlying message that happiness comes from giving to others. Buddhism centers around altruism, which means the selfless concern for others' well-being and not focusing only on ourselves. My husband and I regularly feed the stray cats that live by our house. Food is a basic necessity of all living creatures. When we feed the cats, our intention is to be selfless and to be able to provide for all living things when they are in need or crisis. Of course, by being around them, we are calmer, more grateful and happier, which is an added bonus, but the objective is ensuring they are fed. Gratitude, along with service, is a Buddhist philosophy. We are taught that when we are grateful, we experience instant abundance and the feeling of wanting more no longer exists.

Over a year ago, I decided to seek a lifestyle centered around minimalism. When I was in my early 30s, I splurged and shopped a lot to rediscover my femininity. Maxi dresses, one-piece jumpsuits and high-wedge sandals became an integral part of my wardrobe. I needed to buy as many outfits and espadrilles heels as I could because I was proud of the woman I was becoming.

Now, at my age, I can confidently describe myself as a woman who loves her body and is comfortable in her own skin. I wanted to celebrate owning my feminine side, which I neglected considerably while growing up. But, after doing that for nearly two years, I felt that I didn't need clothes to validate and discover my femininity. I found that my journey had shifted and I was becoming aligned with how I was evolving.

In the beginning, I needed external tools to remind myself that I was womanly. As I dressed in a more stereotypically feminine fashion, I felt increasingly graceful, sensual and elegant. Eventually, femininity became such an integral part of my identity that I didn't need the reminder or to constantly purchase new clothing to feel like a woman. I had become that with time.

A few months ago, I ordered a dinner set online because the ones we had were old and breaking, so we were in dire need of some new cutlery and crockery. Before I placed that order, I didn't know if it was the right thing to do and, for months, I discussed the purchase with my husband. The set, although reasonably priced and affordable, still drove me to think twice and justify to myself why I was buying a new dinner set. Only when I was convinced that I needed it, I placed the order. The tipping point was when I was washing the dishes and noticed cracks in different shapes and angles all over the plates.

I thought I'd be giddy with excitement, but when it arrived I felt nothing. It was then that I learnt how possessions used to control my behavior. The purchase was essential – it adds value to my everyday living, but it is not a source of happiness.

Around that time, I came across the documentary entitled *Minimalism* in which two men, Joshua and Ryan, shared their life story of how they lived high-flying corporate lives, earning six-figure salaries, buying whatever they wanted, and traveling all over the world. Despite all this, they revealed that they felt a deep sense that something was missing and ultimately they weren't happy. As a matter of fact, they were experiencing more misery than when they were younger and living in poor circumstances with their families. I wondered what shifted in them to become minimalist, because I have always been brought up to believe that money equated happiness, especially when Mama was showered with gifts from my dad.

Before he became a minimalist, Ryan believed that "happiness was around the corner", and perpetuated this notion by constantly buying more, seeking newness, and demanding the 'best'. Feeling a gaping void on the inside, he made vain attempts at filling it with more stuff. Consumerism became a way of life. Purchasing more things was similar to buying his way to happiness. As he earned more money, he naturally spent more on mundane items that he didn't need. When Ryan saw his friend, Josh, emanating elation, he was intrigued and asked Josh out for lunch. Ryan blatantly asked him, "Why the hell are you so happy?" Josh shared his experience of living a minimal life that offered him contentment. Josh explained his newfound philosophy. "If something does not add value to your life, then let it go. Get rid of it. It is that simple. The things you own need to have a purpose and you need to be able to justify the possessions you have." It was at that point that Ryan decided to change his lifestyle and, together, they wrote a book and went on tour to promote their ideologies focused on a minimalist way of living.

Ever-changing fashion trends, technology, mass media, advertising and social media bombard us to buy what we see because it looks good. The media has an excellent formula for luring society to obtain – and more often than not, obsess about – the latest items. Advertising campaigns are clever with words, music and imagery that shout out to us, influencing us to buy another new gadget that will supposedly lead to definitive happiness. Many of these items give us a buzz when we buy them, but after a while they just end up in the back of a drawer or closet.

Inspired by the concept of minimalism, I made a conscious decision to question my purchases. This shift in my life was timed perfectly as my husband and I were moving from a three-bedroom apartment with a huge kitchen to a two-bedroom apartment with a kitchen connected to the living room. There was a dire need to downsize as the apartment was about half the size of the previous one. We could have moved to a bigger or same-sized apartment, but we wanted to go minimal so this gave us the chance to put our words into action.

One of the things I started to give away was my snow globe collection. In my early 20s, I began collecting snow globes from each destination I visited. To me, a snow globe is like a magical place, a fantasy in a bubble, in which everything is still and happy. Each time I shook a snow globe, I felt transported to that place, whether it was the clear beach in Santorini or seeing the penguins in Reykjavik in Iceland.

But, I resolved to make an effort to diligently find a new owner for these show pieces.

By the time I revisited my collection, over 50 snow globes stared back at me, showing me a picture perfect distillation of every place I had visited in my life. My heart wanted to give them to someone who would treasure them. After a number of weeks, a collector contacted me and, within that day, they were sold and gone. Out of my home and space. At first I was sad, however a part of me was pleased because I made a choice to let go and to let someone else enjoy the magical experience of these items.

Clothes were much easier to offload from my living space because they didn't hold any sentimental value. I spent months sorting out a pile of garments that had lain dormant in my closet for years. I had a huge pile of giveaways and other items for sale. The interesting experience was, when all my clothes were laid out on the bed, I felt sick! I was disgusted and nauseous at being surrounded by a mountain of fabric. I owned nearly 10 bikinis! I looked at the swimwear and thought, "where did all of these come from? On all of the beach holidays my husband and I have been, I have literally worn two or three, so how did I end up with that many?"

Getting rid of what I wasn't using was such a relief. I felt lighter and I actually enjoyed the mental and physical space that came from de-cluttering. Now, in order to reach the de-cluttering phase faster, I ask myself, "Have I worn this in the past three or four months?" If the answer is no, then out it goes, bearing in mind that the seasons affect my wardrobe choices as well. So, when deciding between giving it away and keeping it, I also think about whether that garment is necessary for a particular season. The key is to always be honest with yourself. The classic lie is, "When I've lost 10 pounds, then I can fit into this dress again. So I better hold onto it as a motivator." That is great, but how honest are we being when we say that? 8 out of 10 times, we aren't, because when we get to the size we've been wanting, to celebrate the hard work we've put in, we go shopping and that beautiful dress that awaits in that tightly-packed closet never gets a second chance.

Over the years, as I turned into a minimalist, I off-loaded tons of clothes, accessories, books and kitchenware from my life. Every day I still work towards becoming more minimal. The less cluttered my house is, the less cluttered my mind is. In the flat we have moved into, I use the spare room to write as we have converted it into a study, whereas in our previous apartment, the spare room was a cluttered storage area. We make it a point to keep this study tidy because I can't write effectively and use the space for inspiration with messy energy. Being a minimalist is a conscious choice because I understand that clutter can cause chaos in the mind. Our surroundings affect us and I now diligently choose to live in a simpler way and within a calmer space. Ultimately, if I own less, I will spend less time on unnecessary decisions. When you have to spend more than 10 minutes deciding what to wear, that amount of time and energy is wasted.

For instance, if one is tired after a long day, it is more likely to cause a reactive decision versus a conscious decision. Fatigue can be mental exhaustion due to the mind having used up most of its energy. Recently, I've been wearing the same clothes every day and I am fine with it. My outfits consist of a tank top or a t-shirt, Aladdin pants and a shawl, depending on the weather. Arianna Huffington discusses how we as women feel the need to change things up and wear something new to look the part at work, but she explains the benefits and importance of repeating ensembles. When we constantly wear something new, we are wasting so much time and energy first thing in the morning over what to wear. On her Instagram account, she hashtags 'repeats' of ensembles to advocate her line of work. Wardrobe anxiety contributes to wasting time, and she thinks we should wear what we love again and again.

Mark Zuckerberg is known to wear grey T shirts. Former President Obama wears his signature blue or grey suits. They deliberately make their outfits 'uniform' because it eradicates the whole process of guessing and figuring out what to wear. In 2017, Obama revealed in a CNN interview that he doesn't want to make choices about what he wears or eats because he has many other decisions to make, which helps him to utilize his energy for things that matter more. I look at these people and emulate some of their lifestyle choices to better use my time and energy to create fruitful and impactful outcomes.

Mindfulness and minimalism go hand-in-hand, similar to a marriage of simplicity. I have seen my life transform through constantly de-cluttering my life. Being happier, wanting to move forward, and constantly clearing up my energy are reasons that drive me to live a minimal life. In practicing the art of being minimal, I have seen the doors open wide to a life full of opportunities, without being tied to the clutter of the past.

After Papa passed away, Big Mama moved from Malaga to Barcelona to live with her younger son. I hadn't seen her for a long time so when I was in the Czech Republic for work in the summer of 2011, I decided to stop over and surprise her. Big Mama wasn't easy to surprise because Bha had to pick me up from the airport and she questioned where he was going on a Sunday. Even though she was in her 80s, she was still in charge, wanting to know what was going on in her family members' lives. Bha had to tell her that his client was in town and he had to meet him.

My earliest recollection of Big Mama was as an elegant woman who dressed immaculately, but the person I saw that summer was very different. As I walked in, I went straight up to her. Everyone was grinning and telling her, "look who's here!" She was ecstatic and couldn't believe her eyes! "Komie, is that really you?" she asked. After my arrival sunk in, she then jokingly pretended to be mad at Bha. "So this is your client!" Everyone laughed.

When I saw her I started weeping uncontrollably. Firstly, because I missed her terribly. Secondly, because she looked simple, very different from how I remembered her.

She was wearing a white *salwar kameez,* which is a traditional Indian outfit that consists of trousers and a long top. Her hair was silver grey. In the past she would dye her hair black religiously to remove any signs of aging. Her nails were unpainted, broken and brittle. Her skin looked dry and my heart ached seeing her in that state. I couldn't understand the dramatic change in her, and it affected me deeply. I simply hadn't seen it coming.

After I had calmed down, my aunt explained that Big Mama was happy and this is how she's been since Papa passed on. I soon realized that she was in a different phase of her life; fancy outfits and matching handbags with sandals didn't matter to her anymore, just like my Barbies and Sweet Valley High novels no longer held the same meaning for me. Big Mama was living a life that was detached from possessions. She was living a minimalist life, but without the label. Some people say that traditional Indian widowers give up on living – the desire to look good no longer serves a purpose when their husbands have died and are no longer in this realm with them. While that may be true, Big Mama was in a unique phase and cared about different things. She spent the extra time she had on God, enjoying her Jelly desserts and the occasional *Two and a Half Men* shows!

Big Mama had chosen to spend less time on her appearance and devoted her limited time to her grandchildren and to God through specific types of prayer. Time with God had allowed her to have more inner peace, happiness and strength. As she was coming to the end of her life, Big Mama was naturally detaching herself from her worldly possessions, just as we learn in Buddhist teachings.

One Buddhist monk I spoke to recently used the analogy of a beautiful holiday. When we go on holiday, we have many things around us (a classy bed, great bath and hopefully top-of the-range catering). We are surrounded by many beautiful things and have a wonderful environment to live in. But when the holiday is over, we move on. We don't consider taking these things with us (unless of course you are a thief). The holiday is finished. It's over.

If you die holding onto what's undone and you stress about it, then you're never going to rest in peace. Big Mama habitually practiced peace and happiness right until the very end. When death came, those around her said that she still had a broad smile on her face. We say to those who are deceased, may they 'rest in peace'. But if we don't practice being in peace whilst we are living, how can we obtain peace during those last few moments? Peace is being content with what *is*.

Limitless

"To be yourself in a world that is constantly trying to make you something else is the greatest accomplishment."

— Ralph Waldo Emerson

One night (when I think I was around 30) I was out with some friends for a night out in Lan Kwai Fong – a small but crazy area of Hong Kong full of bars, clubs and restaurants. It's commonly known as a 'happening' place to party, especially at times of the year like Halloween, when the streets of Lan Kwai Fong are riddled with half-drunk vampires, lecherous werewolves and inappropriately dressed witches. Anyway, on this particular occasion I wasn't a witch but a university student who needed to unwind from the endless essays that I was drowning in. Catching up with old friends at a bar over some mix-and-match cocktails seemed a great way to relax and have some fun. I have always enjoyed people watching and seeing how they communicate and come together, and LKF is the perfect place for that.

I was with some friends at a chic bar drinking a cosmopolitan; we were updating each other on what had been going on in our lives. We would often start with trivial topics, but then as the night evolved we would often move to deeper ones. Most importantly, discussions often revolved around the topic of guys and dating. It is interesting, we all thought, how we can be in a super powerful position at work and yet be muddled and confused when it comes to men and why they don't text or call back. Our night involved unwinding and having a good time. There was some innocent flirting going on with some guys nearby. We had shot after shot of tequila, which doesn't sit well with me. In the company of others on a Friday night, getting a bit tipsy was expected. After a few drinks, I needed the toilet and so I made my way to the ladies room. What happened next surprised me.

It was a cramped toilet with just two cubicles and one sink with an oval mirror above it. The walls were painted in a dull pink hue and it felt like the toilet hadn't been revamped in years. There was one yellow light bulb gently swinging above the sink with barely enough light for someone to wash their hands or to touch up their makeup. In such a congested toilet, I thought I was alone. But on this occasion I was not. As I went out there was a stunning Lebanese girl, a shorter curvier version of Gal Gadot staring at herself in the mirror. She was slightly shorter than me, around 5 feet 4 inches with shoulder-length dark curly hair. There was a slight bounce in her hair when she moved and she had a beautiful smile. Her black, figure-hugging dress accentuated her curves and she had knee-length, black boots on.

She was admiring herself in the mirror, reapplying her make-up. While I'm sometimes a girly girl, I usually don't do this enough. I tend to wear make-up in the morning and, if it doesn't last me all day, I'm fine with it. I liked seeing her put on her wine-red MAC lipstick. I found myself transfixed by her slow actions and her stunning beauty. After a few seconds, I composed myself and made my way to the only sink in the toilet. After she was done with her lipstick, she turned and my face was right in front of hers. It seemed almost instinctive that our lips would come together. We were suddenly inexplicably engaged in a full throttle French kiss; our lips were locked and it didn't feel in the least bit awkward. In fact it felt natural as our bodies entwined, rubbed and grinded together. The kiss went on for some time and our hands extended to our breasts and thighs. It was clearly getting steamy and we were both feeling the heat. I stroked her dark, olive skin and I heard her respond with a small moan of pleasure. My hand moved up and down her thigh as I began to take charge of the situation. She responded with soft sighs and purrs of appreciation. After what seemed an age we disentangled and smiled gently to one another. I left the bathroom with an extra bounce in my feet and a million-dollar smile. It was only afterwards that I discovered we had mutual friends and that this olive-skinned beauty was named Kitana.

I remember walking up to my friend and telling her that I "kissed a girl, and I liked it." I was laughing because I was in a state of shock and was only just comprehending what had just happened. I wanted to make light of what had just occurred. My friend told me that, considering my attitude towards other 'norms' dictated by my culture, she wasn't in the least bit surprised.

I haven't thought much about that incident since the time that it happened. I haven't made out with another girl since Kitana so I never really labeled myself as bisexual. But, as I was thinking about my identity and the experiences I have had in my younger years, this encounter with Kitana struck me deeply. To obtain a clearer understanding of my identity, I had a chat with my childhood friend, Amy. She knows me well and I thought, "why not ask her about this side of me?" In her opinion, I wasn't bisexual at all. Instinctive curiosity may have led to my experiences with women. While I may have thoroughly enjoyed it, I never thought of women when I lay in bed – it was always men. "Being intrigued to know yourself more, you experimented but it doesn't label you automatically as bisexual," she added. With that in mind, it made more sense that I was open to exploring. Deep-down, I know that I am heterosexual.

As an Indian girl, I wasn't exposed to sexuality other than what was taught in school – or through my father's actions – which was incredibly limiting. Even though I had a childhood in which I was introduced forcefully to sex, there was – and still is – a taboo about openly talking about sex or sexuality in my community. My limited exposure in childhood made me assume I was heterosexual, and the possibility to dive into bisexuality never even occurred to me. Luckily, I had a taste of what lesbianism felt like, if only for a brief moment.

Writing this memoir has allowed me to dig deep into my own journey through life. As I write, I am learning and noticing a lot more about the person I was and the limitless opportunities of who I can be. I am privileged, or perhaps even brave, to have been able to entertain thoughts of bisexuality because I do not let my cultural upbringing become a wall blinding me from my own self-exploration anymore.

Let's go back to the rendez-vous I had with Kitana. That amazing opportunity was spontaneous without any degree of forethought. Pure spontaneity is rare for me but on that occasion it felt very right. I knew I was attracted to her so I acted upon that primal instinct at that specific moment. I took a risk and I found out it was well worth it. I didn't cave in or shy away due to taboos or fear of the unknown. I enjoyed the encounter we had and it allowed me to think about my own sexual preferences. It also made me consider the types of relationships I wanted in the future.

The fact that I am able to be vocal, sharing these parts of my life: sex, forced sex (rape/incest) and sexuality, makes me strongly believe that these subjects need to be addressed. It is my hope that sharing my story allows others in my culture to be more open with their dialogue within the community.

* * *

Over the years, I had become a kind of unofficial psychologist to my friends, who would call me when they had tears to shed, relationships to pick apart and examine, or confessions to divulge. Once, a good friend of mine came over and told me about a man she had been seeing, and I couldn't believe how distressed she was.

As she cried, and told me the details about what had been going on, I felt alarm bells going off in my head.

"He just doesn't get back to me."

"One minute he is totally into me, and the next he is gone."

"I just feel like I am giving so much, and getting nothing back."

I felt like I had heard this, all of this, before. But it had come from me. Only a few years before, I had been in a similar turmoil, about one of a string of random guys, and I felt so out of control of the relationship that I could have gone crazy. Here was my friend, echoing the same exact sentiments right back at me, devastated and sobbing.

It was like looking in a mirror. She kept telling me about all the effort she was putting into the relationship, how he wanted to give him the benefit of the doubt and give him another chance, that if only she could be different, if only she had done something different, if only...

It was in that moment that I could see that it wasn't this relationship that was the problem, or even that useless guy. My friend needed help. She needed help to see that she couldn't fix a relationship that was unfixable to begin with. I saw each of her cries as testament to her extremely low self-esteem, and I could relate.

And then, I knew. I needed to find a way to train myself, so that I could truly have the skills and tools to help others, not just my friends, but anyone who needed support in the way I had received it, and was now giving it to my friend. Soon after, I came across an advertisement for a counseling course offered by Monash University in Australia, and I signed up without another thought.

Since I completed the course, I have been working as a counselor specializing in trauma and relationships, and I have found that it's just another string to add to my bow. It has informed my teaching, my work with students on the debate team, and has opened doors for what I am able to contribute to society and my community in an incredible way.

* * *

A year ago, I saw a post on a Facebook group by a friend looking to interview people for her podcast, Hong Kong Confidential. Jules Hannaford's aim is to provide a space in which people can share their stories of struggle and how they have overcome adversity. When I saw her message, I decided to contact her. I have a story, and it was time I shared what I had gone through as a child.

We met and, to my surprise, I was at ease and comfortable talking to her about my experience of having gone through incest. She was interested in my journey as a whole and her constant compassion during the interview helped me to expose more about what happened. We talked about what I had experienced, how I coped with it and, more importantly, how my life has changed for the better today. Her platform was an avenue for me to share my story so people can realize that rape or incest doesn't have to limit them in any way. Life moves on, and through forgiveness as well as acceptance, one can change the way they feel.

One of the topics we talked about on the podcast was arranged marriage. This is by no means saying arranged marriages don't work. It simply wasn't the route for me. And honestly, I was too young to understand what was right for me, let alone make a decision about marriage at such a young age. I told her that I can now safely say that I know what I didn't want. I talked about how I went to India to be 'arranged' and went through the motions and knew deep down that I wasn't going to meet 'the one' at that point.

The trip to India wasn't wrong in itself, but it wasn't right for me. I felt I had to fit a certain mold, which I inevitably wasn't able to fit. After Jules and I talked about the India trip fiasco, we went to the heart of the issue: incest. We discussed how my father was excessively into sex and that he is a 'preferred sex offender'. We talked about how, as an Indian woman, it was my duty to please my man when I got married. I told her that my father said he was 'teaching me' the ropes and assuring me that I was still a virgin, when in actuality I wasn't. I believed his words as if they were holy scriptures and it affected my relationship with men. I constantly feared I wasn't good enough when I was dating men and it sabotaged many relationships. Being unaware of how a family should be or what the role of parents was, I explained, I accepted what I got because every child like me wanted to be loved. I could finally articulate that now, my idea of love comes from compassion, care, commitment and being unique.

Publicly sharing my story about something as personal as incest was the hardest thing I had ever done. The need to express my feelings and the events of my life through a friend's podcast was not only for me, because this kind of trauma is happening to children every day. I hoped my story would at least bring some comfort to those going through what I had endured. My story is the story of many girls who've grown up feeling broken, lacking confidence, and feeling utterly lost because of abuse or incest. Sharing my story allowed me to let the listeners on Jules' podcast know that rape does happen, even with people we trust. My message was: know that even something as horrific as incest does not limit how your life unfolds as long as you stay with the difficult task of working through the repercussions and getting the help that is needed.

Months after the original podcast was aired, we did another podcast in which I talked about the work I do in trauma and relationship therapy and how Arlene Drake's book, *Carefrontation,* is my personal and professional toolkit when I am seeking clarification on certain issues. Arlene uses a lot of inner-child work, but also provides practical exercises that assist adult survivors to heal from wounds from their childhood. My aim in sharing and spreading this knowledge is to equip people who have suffered to reconnect with that little child in them, so they too can come full circle and not live with the pain of haunting past experiences.

Telling my story on the podcasts was liberating because I was finally on a virtual platform talking about something that many are afraid to discuss. The shame attached to rape is so high that many fear speaking up. As an Indian, when my country has such high incidences of rape, I feel it is my responsibility to help break that silence with the hope to empower more women to speak up and get the support they need and deserve.

In December, another opportunity presented itself. This was in conjunction with the #MeToo scandal that hit the US in October 2017. In Hong Kong, it became the talk of the town a few months after. Social media was flooded with #MeToo comments and posts and it became one of the most covered stories in history.

Sexual harassment is a social problem that men and women face all around the world. Statistically, far more women go through inappropriate sexual advances, whether in a workplace, university, or at home.

When all of this was going on, I came across an event called, "#MeToo, Now What?" I was intrigued and felt it was the right time for me to be a part of it. I never knew that it would open so many doors and give me a chance to share how to address and curb sexual harassment within the community. I spoke to Karen See of Embrace Worldwide about my interest in this event. Karen initiated this movement with Helen Lockey from The University of Hong Kong and together with Keshia Hannam of Camel Assembly, they ventured into starting this movement in Hong Kong to create a safe space for women and men to identify, respond to and end sexual harassment. The moment I saw the event page, I knew I had something to offer professionally and also personally. I explained to Karen my background and how I could contribute to this movement. Before I knew it, I was on the panel as the trauma and relationship counselor for the first event, which was being held that very week.

Many perpetrators of sexual harassment are unaware of the impact or implications that their actions cause to their victims. They are ignorant of how sexist comments, sleazy stares, or an inappropriate action or word affects victims. Women have been seen as sex objects within most cultures for centuries. Today, women throughout the world are speaking up. On some occasions this has confused the perpetrators of sexual harassment. Why is it a problem now when it wasn't a problem in the past? As a matter of fact, it was always a problem but because of a power dynamic chronically tipped out of women's favor, a lack of education on the subject and the rigidly patriarchal world we live in, many women dared not speak up.

Today, there is a greater consciousness that sexual harassment and abuse are unacceptable and will not be swept under the carpet. More and more women are standing up and learning to identify and respond to sexual harassment. This is vital step so that we can be able to begin to curb the issue.

With the gravity of this situation in mind, I spoke at the #MeToo, Now What? event from a place of being pro-men. Throughout history and in most cultures, men have undeniably had more power than women. So, women have inevitably been the victims of sexual harassment. Blaming men for the issue fails to eradicate the problem. It simply separates men from women and creates more tension between the sexes. Sinking into the mindset that men are evil and we are the weaker gender, does not serve anyone. Ultimately, both men and women want to be loved and respected. It is only through working with men rather than working against them that a solution can be found.

At the end of the event, one of the participants, Fiona, came up to me with a quandary. She said that she was glad she came to the event because she found it practical and the takeaways gave her food for thought. Earlier in the day, she had a chance, during a group coaching session, to listen to other people's stories, which helped her understand what constitutes sexual harassment. It was a session for the participants to be guided by a facilitator who was a coach, a counselor, or psychologist, to share their stories if they wanted to, or discuss some of the questions they had in mind.

Bolstered by the vulnerable shares she had witnessed by her peers in the coaching session, she shared her story of how her supervisor's actions made her uncomfortable. One day, her supervisor was leaning in when she was using her laptop. Fiona found herself feeling uneasy but didn't know what to do. She worried that she'd appear petty by speaking up about the issue. She also didn't want to make a mountain out of a molehill. One of the panelist firmly suggested that Fiona tell her supervisor to stop doing what he was doing. She told Fiona that she needed to make it clear that it made her uncomfortable. Fiona replied that she was new in her job and felt that course of action was too risky. The result was that she was left in a quandary about what to do.

Later on, as we discussed it together, I tried to come up with a suggestion that would allow Fiona to make her point in a less direct way, since I knew firsthand how frightening it could be to be in a new job! I suggested that the next time he was getting too close, and invading her space, she could physically move away from him, by either getting up and moving, or turning away pointedly. Hopefully, I thought, by moving away, her supervisor would get the hint. If the situation continued she could then say something about it.

I said, "if you're feeling uncomfortable and not 100 percent sure about the situation or his intentions, then you need to call him out and say that his actions are making you uncomfortable." I told her to let him know what he had done without getting emotional or subjective, to stick with the facts and say it calmly. The intention is to ensure that such behavior stops so how we communicate is vital. I continued to say, "Use the calm and collected approach and let him know so he's aware of his actions. If it persists, then he has been warned. And then you can take a firm stance, as well as action against him if he doesn't stop. Because no, means no." And finally, if the situation continued to deteriorate she could also contact HR.

The event was a success not only because we had a huge turnout, but because the women who attended were able to reflect on what they discovered about sexual harassment and how to best respond to it. Our goal is to equip participants with a basic toolkit so they are empowered and are able to address inappropriate sexual situations without panicking.

Ultimately, it is learning to take a stand and to know what to do in an incident when they feel uncomfortable or violated. Our first event was aimed at helping women to recognize that this problem exists and that there is a safe space to speak about their concerns and explore solutions to tackle harassment. But, we believe that men too needed to be a part of this dialogue in order to bring awareness to them. Our aim was to galvanize us all to work towards a common goal, and end harassment, as well as opening the doors to communication hence we organized our next event, which included men.

At this event, consent became a topic of discussion. When raising kids, they are touched, fed, and bathed, which involves physical contact. Permission isn't asked. This goes on to when we have a visiting uncle and we ask our daughter to hug him and she doesn't want to. We decide she is being rude and we insist. We are telling her that her feelings are wrong and that she needs to ignore them and obey. Modeling and valuing consent for children from an early age is paramount because, when they are older, if any inappropriate behavior is directed towards them they would be well aware of their own boundaries and confident to say 'no.' When a habit to speak up when something is wrong is instilled from an early age, children will be more likely to voice when they are uncomfortable.

The participants, both men and women, expressed how they felt a space like this helped in understanding what the subtleties of sexual harassment are and, by sharing them, it helped to clarify what was acceptable and unacceptable behavior.

In March, we had an event for the Indian community and called it, *Desi (Indian) #MeToo, Now What?* I ran this event because it was something I had wanted to push for in Hong Kong for many years. I felt there was a dire need to address sexual harassment in the home. The previous events were geared towards the workplace. However, this particular one was focused on home and social aspects as sexual harassment amongst Indian communities rarely occur in the workplace. Many participants were initially skeptical about the need to be informed about sexual harassment, especially when they had never encountered such an experience. But upon attending, quite a number of them shared how they had no clue that sexual harassment can take place in university, in clubs, or at a friend's house party. As many of the participants were parents, this opened their eyes to how little they knew about what could happen to their children if they were not educated on the importance of having a voice, and drawing clear boundaries in their lives.

There is a huge need for more Indian parents to attend so that their children can be informed and made aware of the damaging implications and actions of sexual harassment. Our mission at the event was to educate people on how to respond when you are facing it.

My ultimate aim is to know that, when I leave this world, I have made an impact. Knowing that many lives have been changed for the better because of the work I do would be the best gift I can receive. Although I know I have worked hard to move through the repercussions of the immense challenges I have faced, I know the strong backbone of my vision, perseverance and faith comes from a very special source: I am honored to have had a remarkable woman like my grandmother in my life. She has shown me the essence of being limitless in a world sometimes void of compassion. It is because of her I have written this book and can finally tell my story.

Owning My Story

"There is no greater agony than bearing an untold story inside you."

— Maya Angelou

When I was 23, my father walked away from our family, leaving my mom, brother and I with barely any money or any degree of financial support. We very nearly lost everything. Though it seemed sudden to those in the local community, this had been coming for some time. My father had been living in two different realities for some time. I never understood why he couldn't be honest about it instead of living two separate and very different lives. But as I got older, I realized that he was afraid. His fear led him to suppressing his ability to speak up and say what he was truly feeling. He was unwilling or unable to face our reactions. So rather than face up to our reactions, he walked away.

We don't learn in school or university to overcome the awkwardness of confrontation, yet confrontation is necessary in the world we live in. Sometimes people need to hear what they don't want to hear, even when it hurts. When a person leaves without confrontation, it can leave devastation in their wake.

I'm learning that when people haven't owned their stories, they can feel awkward and uncertain. They are uncomfortable dealing with conflict and aren't able to truly connect with people on a deeper level. This insecurity can often lead to irrational and destructive patterns of thinking and behavior. This destructive behavior not only impacts those around them, but also themselves.

The ability to own our stories necessarily comes with vulnerability and discomfort. To be real, and honest, with ourselves about our history, regrets, and wounds, necessitates a strong sense of self. If we can know for certain, that no matter what happens, we will end up okay, there is very little in life we won't be able to meet head-on. There is no story we wouldn't be able to take ownership of. Following is a summary of the long and winding road I took towards being able to own mine.

Ten years ago, I began to unpack the pandora's box of what I had been through, in therapy. I didn't even know the extent of the ways I had been mistreated when I went in, and a huge part of my initial journey through therapy was acceptance and understanding of what happened to me. Only then could I begin to process the unseen emotions, memories and beliefs that came with such an immense violation since such a young age. I came out the other side with more clarity, self-assuredness and a deep connection to my own ability to be strong in the face of adversity.

Five years ago, I finally decided (after much consternation) to tell my family about what I had lived through. I was not going to remain uncommunicative about it or walk away like it had never happened. I felt like I no longer needed to live a lie. Removing the mask I had worn for so long revealed my vulnerability and that was one of the scariest experiences of my life. Fears of all kinds ran through my mind and gripped at my breath in my chest. I was terrified they would reject me – I would lose my family and become even more alienated than I already was. I was afraid that they wouldn't believe me because I'd been quiet for so many years. In my late 30s, I couldn't keep it to myself any longer, and I am glad to say that my family made the decision to stand beside me.

Three years ago, after some years of study and practice, I converted to Buddhism. It was through the sensitivity and grace of the teachings and contemplative practices that I found elements of peace and acceptance that I did not even know I was looking for. I connected deeply with the gift of forgiveness and know firsthand the beauty in connecting to meditation on loving-kindness. Through my studies in Buddhism, I feel able to integrate the stories of my past gently back into my present.

Over a year ago, I plucked up the courage to speak about my childhood trauma on a podcast. On this virtual platform, anyone, anywhere in the world would have access to my story. Taking that step was nerve-wracking, but I knew that if I wanted to inspire other people to do the same, I had to speak up. I shared all the details of my traumatic childhood and to my surprise a number of women and men from around the world got in touch with me. I realized I could make an impact and it motivated me to be a voice for those that had been sexually abused. After being on the podcast, I felt more empowered and felt that I had done the right thing. Since then, I have become more comfortable talking about sexual harassment and the impact it has on survivors of traumatic events.

I didn't participate in the podcast to draw attention to myself. I wanted to be able to speak up and give a voice so that other survivors could own their story. I knew a deep sense of healing took place for me when I no longer had to pretend I had a 'normal' childhood. Opening up about the trauma I endured while giving myself permission to be real and honest catapulted me towards acceptance of myself for the way I am.

Riding the wave of the feeling of freedom and success I had gained by speaking on the podcast, I embarked on what would perhaps be the greatest test of my ability to own my story: writing this book. Writing something down is inherently cathartic, and always allows a fresh perspective. I began to see just how far I had come, how much I had transformed – I truly was like the lotus flower, striving ever upward towards the light.

Big Mama was expressive and had no qualms about speaking her mind, even when it might go against the beliefs or opinions of others. She would tell me she loved me and wasn't scared of expressing that love. When I did something that wasn't up to her standard, she made a point to let me know. She was never one who shied away from saying what she was thinking! I remember her saying to me once, "if I don't tell you, you will never know. I rather it be me that tells you what isn't right because you are my granddaughter. But if someone else criticizes you, it would hurt me because I know my intention. I can't speak for others."

She taught me that when we confront a person and tell them how we feel, our intention is what matters. How we say it makes all the difference.

It doesn't mean it won't hurt if something that we are expressing is emotionally difficult but we are aware that we are being true to ourselves and we are also being responsible in communicating what is going on instead of keeping the person in the dark. When I was a child, I was shy and would never speak up.

A Girl's Faith has given me the courage to understand that I can't change what has happened to me as an incest survivor. What I know is that Big Mama's teachings gave me hope that there is life beyond pain and suffering. Her wisdom is locked in my DNA and no one can change that. I stand as a pioneer for other women to use their voice as a means to communicate their feelings. And as Big Mama has taught me, it is how we use our voices that reflects who we are. It is with her blessing that I have written this book, and I know she is in heaven smiling at me for my courage. I urge all of the women and men out there who have been abused to speak your truth, own your life, and know that there are always people out there who are ready to hear your story, help you through it and support you as you heal.

Why I Wrote A Girl's Faith

It took me a long time to decide to write *A Girl's Faith*. I wanted to write it from a place of strength, understanding, compassion and empathy rather than a place of revenge or anger. I wasn't going to write this book until I found the ability to be in that space. *A Girl's Faith* is about my journey and the shift I have made to become the woman I am today, and the woman I will hopefully become tomorrow. The main focus of *A Girl's Faith* is on forgiveness, which I highlight at the end of the book.

This book isn't about pointing the finger at who wasn't there for me during those times because that will never change. Several years ago, I underwent quite extensive therapy. After therapy and when I was in a different mental place, I was able to confront my mother and father and speak my truth. It took courage to tell my family and my extended family that I had been raped and molested over a number of years, by my father.

My mom said I was responsible for the rape and molestation due to what she perceived as the close bond I had with my father. After I told my immediate family I took it upon myself to message my father's second wife, Sharon, and their daughter. I did this not out of spite, but because I wanted them to know what had happened to me. I was afraid the same thing might have happened to my half-sister, Rani. I have to acknowledge that I never heard back from Rani or Sharon. After I revealed what happened to me, my father apologized by text and I could then use that as proof when explaining the circumstances to my extended family.

Some people have asked if I ever considered pressing legal charges against my father. The answer is yes; I have entertained the possibility and even went so far as to speak to a lawyer who is an expert in this area. I weighed up all the options and decided that I wanted to take control of my life and not spend any more time being stuck in a cycle of hurt. It was during this period in my life that I came across my main Buddhist teacher. He has taught me loving-kindness meditation, which I now use every day. He has also imparted important knowledge on how to forgive but still have boundaries.

I do not carry anger in me today. That has been the choice I have made for myself. I have chosen to live in the present and not let the past define who I am. This allows me the privilege of being able to look forward to the future with a sense of hope. The shift in my decision not to harbor any anger and pain is a result of knowing that I have control over my actions, decisions and relationships which are all based in the now, and do not have to be colored by my past.

Those who meet me know I radiate life and happiness. However, this was not always the case. There was a dark time in my life when I was stuck in pain; looking continually dull, drained and devoid of life. Today I no longer feel that energy because I have let go from within. *A Girl's Faith* is about my journey and how I'm living my life despite what happened. It is also about who I have chosen to become.

I am a survivor and not a victim.

"I love the person I have become, because I fought to become her."

— Kaci Diane

About The Author

Meet Karina:

Karina is a qualified counselor from Monash University, Australia, specializing in Trauma and Relationship counseling.

She uses Solution Focused Brief Therapy (SFBT), Cognitive Behavioral Therapy (CBT), as well as Mindfulness based Cognitive Therapy (MBCT), with clients who have experienced trauma or have issues in distressed relationships.

Her first love is teaching and she obtained two degrees from the University of Hong Kong in 2008 and 2011. Her first degree was a Bachelor of Education (B.Ed.) and the second, a Master's in Fine Arts (MFA) in creative writing.

Over the last decade, Karina has integrated her qualifications into her life and her passion for teaching and coaching debate tournaments, which has enhanced her profession as a teacher.

Her love for counseling stems from the fact that she has been a shoulder to lean on for many friends, students and clients. Karina has seen a therapist and realizes that integrating this into her teaching assists students to cope with their struggles. As a high school teacher, Karina empathizes with the pressures some students endure during their formative years.

When she was a teenager, Karina began writing poetry and essays and a few years ago, she started a series of blogs. This led to a variety of opportunities, including writing her memoir entitled *A Girl's Faith,* which is dedicated to her Grandma who passed away in 2018. More importantly, her memoir uncovers her experiences as a rape survivor.

Her story, told through *A Girl's Faith,* has led her to assist women with *#MeToo* events in Hong Kong, which has allowed Karina to create a platform where women can talk freely and confidentially about their experiences while finding tools to cope with their struggles.

As a vegan, minimalist and a Buddhist, Karina lives by the motto of being the best version of herself by embodying a simple and mindful life.

A Girl's Faith – A Memoir by Karina Calver

Synopsis

Karina is an Indian woman, born into a middle-class Sindhi family in Hong Kong, who reveals her journey of being a rape survivor and how she coped with abuse at the hands of an adult who misused his power. Her story exposes how she overcame the solitude she felt as a child. Unwilling to remain defined by her past, Karina ultimately became a survivor.

Karina's bravery is highlighted in her story as she shares aspects of a life that many don't have the courage to talk about. In her memoir, she unmasks her truth after living with an untold story for so many years. Until she found the guidance and support she needed, she was then able to move forward as an adult.

A Girl's Faith walks us through Karina's religious practices, cultural nuances, expectations, dating experiences, close bond with her beloved Grandma, and her high-school teacher, to whom she first revealed this secret. She reveals the relationship she had with her maiden name; Komal, and a conscious decision to change her identity, in order to emerge from the muddy water like a lotus flower.

A Girl's Faith will transport you into Karina's world from being a rape survivor, to a teacher, a trauma counselor and now a published author. Her short stories, dedicated to her grandmother, uncloak how Karina managed to eradicate stereotypes, learn about deep forgiveness, and challenge herself to tell her story.

My Vegan Life – Passed Down Recipes!

Food was one of the ways our families came together – it brought laughter, chats and happy moments. Growing up, there was always food being cooked and here are some of my favorite childhood recipes that have been passed down from my grandma. Happy cooking!

"Food, just like love is the ingredient that brings people together."

– Karina Calver

Masala Toast

Ingredients:

1 onion, finely chopped
1 tomato, finely chopped
a handful of coriander, finely chopped
half a cup vegan daiya shredded mozzarella cheese (or as much as you like!)
vegan butter (I use avocado spread from Marks & Spencer)
whole grain or whole wheat sliced bread
salt and pepper (optional)

Method:

On 2 slices of bread, spread the vegan butter of your choice.
In a bowl, mix the finely chopped ingredients. Mix well.
Add the shredded cheese to the bowl and continue to mix until all the ingredients are mixed well.
Using a spoon, spread the mixture onto the buttered slices of bread.
Add salt and pepper if you want. Place the bread slices in an oven to toast.
Once it is slightly brown, your masala toast is ready.
This is a typical breakfast on a lazy weekend over a cup of chai.

Saibhaji (Spinach Lentil Stew)

Ingredients:

1 cup spinach

1 cup of split chickpea

¾ big onion

3 tomatoes

2 pcs green chilies

½ pc carrot

½ pc eggplant

½ potato

½ tsp turmeric

1 inch of shaved ginger

15 cloves of garlic

1 tsp chili powder

salt

1 tsp frozen or fresh fenugreek leaves

½ glass water

½ cup of tamarind juice

Method:

Soak split chickpea for at least 5-6 hours.

Use a pressure cooker, add oil then sauté onion until it is light pink.

Add split chickpea, sauté for 5-10 mins.

Add all vegetables (potato, carrot, eggplant, spinach), fenugreek, sauté for 5 mins.

Add tomatoes, green chilies, salt, ginger, water and let the pressure cooker release 7-8 whistles.

When it has cooled down, use a masher to mash all the vegetables (don't use a blender because it will become a liquid-substance).

Add tamarind juice to the mixture, and boil for (10 mins).

Add sautéed garlic (which needs to be done in a separate frying pan with some oil until it is golden brown) and red chili powder.

Mix all ingredients together.

Turn off the stove and your saibhaji is ready!

Dal Pakwan (Lentil Curry With Deep-fried Bread)

Dal ingredients:

250 gram split chickpea
1 small onion
1 small tomato
3 green chilies
1 tsp cumin seeds
5 or 6 curry leaves
3 cups water
½ tsp turmeric powder
2 tsp oil
A pinch of asafoetida
Salt to taste

Method:

Wash split chickpeas and soak for an hour.
Pour 2 tsp. oil in a pressure cooker and allow it to heat.
Add asafoetida, chopped onion and fry for a couple of minutes.
Add grated tomato and fry until cooked.
Add split chickpea, turmeric powder and salt.
Add a little water and close lid of pressure cooker.
Wait for one whistle.
Open lid, check the lentil. It should be tender, but not mushy.
t 1 tsp of oil in another pan and prepare a tempering of cumin seeds and curry leaves.
Add the tempering to lentil. Let it simmer for a while.
While serving, sprinkle mango powder, chili powder, coriander leaves.
Serve hot with crisp Pakwan.

Pakwan (deep-fried tortilla-looking bread)

Ingredients:

2 cups all-purpose flour

½ tsp cumin seeds/ caraway seeds either or both

3 tbsp oil

Salt to taste

½ tsp red chili powder

sufficient water to make a dough

oil for deep frying

Method:

Sieve the flour.

Mix the flour with the cumin seeds, caraway seeds, oil, salt and sufficient water and make a dough. Dough should neither be too hard nor too soft. Let the dough rest for 15 min.

Later, divide the dough into 10 small portions. Roll out each portion like a chapatti.

Prick the surface with fork, so that it doesn't puff out (don't forget to do this). Heat the oil until smoking, slide in the Pakwan and carefully fry on medium or low flame until till crisp and golden in color.

Serve with hot dal.

Sindhi Loli (Whole Wheat Bread With Spices)

Ingredients:

3 cups wheat flour

½ tsp salt

1 tsp cracked coriander seeds

1 tsp carom seeds

½ tsp mango powder

½ red onion

¾ cup fresh coriander leaves, minced

1 chili, minced

4 tbsp olive oil

Enough warm water to pull dough together

Bit of flour to roll out dough

Oil to pan fry

Method:

Combine the flour with salt in a large bowl.

Add the rest of the ingredients, except the liquids, mixing it all together.

Drizzle in the olive oil, rub into the flour with the tip of your fingers.

Add warm water, a tablespoon at a time, pulling the dough together.

Do not knead or over mix. It will be slightly sticky, but that's fine because you'll dredge it.

On a surface, place ½ cup of flour and some on the rolling out area.

Divide the dough into 8, shaping it into a small balls with slightly oiled palms.

Coat the balls in flour and roll each into a circle 2-3mm in thickness.

Heat a non-stick pan and sprinkle some drops of oil, waiting for it to sizzle before introducing the loli.

When the edges begin to dry and the bottom is cooked, sprinkle a few drops of oil on the top side before flipping it over to cook completely.

Repeat with remaining dough.

There you have your loli!

Vegan Japanese Curry

Ingredients:

½ onion, thinly sliced

4 cloves of garlic, finely chopped

1 tbsp ginger, finely chopped

1 tbsp flour

2 to 3 tsp curry powder

¼ tsp turmeric

1¼ cup chopped carrots

1 large potato, cubed

2 tsp tomato paste

2 tsp soy sauce

2 cups water

¾ tsp salt

3 tbsp applesauce

⅓ cup peas

oil

Note: another option is to use S&B curry cube. There is a vegan one. Then you can omit curry powder, turmeric, applesauce, tomato paste, soy sauce and flour.

Method:

In a pressure cooker, add oil.

When oil is hot, add onion and pinch of salt and cook until translucent.

Add garlic and ginger and mix. Cook for half a minute.

Move onions to the side.

Add 1 tsp more oil to the pot, add the flour and mix into the oil. Then mix with the onion, ginger, garlic and cook for half a minute, stirring frequently as the flour will tend to stick and burn if left too long.

Add the spices and mix them in.

Add the veggies, sauces, salt and water. Mix really well to pick up the roasted flour from the bottom, so that none of the flour is sticking.

Pressure cook for 6 to 7 minutes. Once the time is up, let pressure release naturally.

Open the lid, add the applesauce and peas and bring to a boil.

Taste and adjust salt, spice and flavor carefully. Add more spices to taste.

Serve with steamed rice.

Where To Find Karina Calver

- www.karinacalver.com
- Where to buy *A Girl's Faith*: Amazon
- www.facebook.com/agirlsfaith

Resources

Langevin R, Wortzman G, Wright P &Handy L.
(1989) Studies of brain damage and dysfunction in sex
offenders. *Annals of Sex Research*; 2, pp. 163- 179

Lanning, V. K. (2010) Child Molesters. A Behavioral
Analysis. For Professional Investigating the Sexual
Exploitation of Children. *National Center for Missing and
Exploited Children. U.S. Department of Justice.* pp. 1-212.

The Mayo Clinic. (2018, March 17). Irritable Bowel
Syndrome. Retrieved from https://www.mayoclinic.org/
diseases-conditions/irritable-bowel-syndrome/symptoms-
causes/syc-2036001